Praise for
The Employee Engagement Mindset

"These insightful and practical solutions get to the heart of employee engagement—the individual. The six drivers of high engagement ring true from personal experience. Organizations and individuals expecting meaningful improvement will embrace this mindset shift."
> —Tyler England, director of Customer Insight, Hewlett-Packard Company

"*The Engagement Mindset* makes it clear that successful engagement is *not* a spectator sport. In today's always-connected world, real and effective personal engagement is more important than ever."
> —Major General (Ret.) Craig Bambrough, former deputy commanding
> general, U.S. Army Reserve Command

"High engagement can spring from only one source: employees who are more than workers and roles that are more than jobs. With extraordinary lucidness, this book teaches us the principles underlying this new reality. It is illumination in the wilderness. A brilliant work!"
> —Ronald D. Maines, attorney; cocreator of The History Channel;
> adjunct professor, Georgetown University; senior visiting fellow,
> Cambridge University

"Some say that managers should *give* people pride in their work. My parents would have scoffed at that; they believed that one *takes* pride in one's work. That notion is also the premise of this practical guide on how to survive and thrive in the global workplace."
> —Mette Norgaard, coauthor of *TouchPoints*

"While the notion of engagement has been around a long time, this book both underscores its importance and gives timely guidance to the leader as to what to do to get it. This one is worth reading, thinking about, and doing something about. It's a keeper."
> —Eric Denna, chief information officer, University of Utah

"This book should come with a warning label: 'Warning: Allocate time and alert your family! You will not be able to put the book down until you finish it!'"

—Jeffrey D. Clark, chief executive officer, JD Clark & Associates

"As nonprofit leaders, we sometimes mistakenly think that our altruistic missions alone will engage our employees. This book can be a great companion to our leadership if we can incorporate the six drivers of employee engagement to support our people in achieving real emotional commitment to their work."

—Annette Royle-Mitchell, president, National MS Society,
Utah-Southern Idaho Chapter

"*The Employee Engagement Mindset* is crucial to what we need in today's workforce. Understanding and living the six drivers will be essential to the success of both the employee and leader in the twenty-first century."

—William A. Inglis, president, Slideworks, Inc.

"Wow! I am impressed. The message of *The Employee Engagement Mindset* is so relevant for the times we are in. Never before have I felt as if there are so many people walking around feeling like victims rather than taking personal responsibility for their situation. This book is terrific! It is a breath of fresh air!"

—Chris Harrison, senior vice president, Robson Communities

"This book is a wonderful reminder that true engagement comes from the inside out. *The Employee Engagement Mindset* provides both rich food for thought and a road map to outstanding results. An insightful and informative read."

—Alan Fine, founder and president, InsideOut Development

The
Employee
Engagement
Mindset

THE SIX DRIVERS FOR TAPPING INTO THE HIDDEN POTENTIAL OF EVERYONE IN YOUR COMPANY

TIMOTHY R. CLARK

New York   Chicago   San Francisco   Lisbon   London
Madrid   Mexico City   Milan   New Delhi   San Juan
Seoul   Singapore   Sydney   Toronto

1 2 3 4 5 6 7 8 9 10   QFR/QFR   1 8 7 6 5 4 3 2

ISBN   978-0-07-178829-8
MHID   0-07-178829-8

e-ISBN   978-0-07-178830-4
e-MHID   0-07-178830-1

McGraw-Hill books are available at special quantity discounts to use as premiums and sales promotions or for use in corporate training programs. To contact a representative, please e-mail us at bulksales@mcgraw-hill.com.

This book is printed on acid-free paper.

For Tracey Clark, Yvonne Clarke Gottfredson, Donna Lyman, Cherise Holley Cragun, Cindi Savage, Lori Baer, Claudia Kiefer, and Kathy Aitchison

Contents

1

Who Owns Your Engagement?

"Life leaps like a geyser for those willing to drill through the rock of inertia."

Alexis Carrel

In first grade she woke up in the morning, dressed in stretch pants and a bright paisley shirt, gave her hair a quick run-through with the comb, and then stood for inspection before her older siblings. On the way to school, she rolled down the hill, gathering up grass, leaves, and burrs. After dusting off, she walked into the classroom and found her desk. No one said anything until the report card came. "I always got an unsatisfactory mark for 'comes to school neat and clean,'" she points out. "It drove my mother crazy."

That's not a remarkable story until you learn that Lois Collins's parents were both blind. They knew people would cut their children slack if they didn't perform to a socially acceptable standard. There would always be an out if they needed it. But her parents emphatically rejected that idea. "They taught us just the opposite. We had no hired help at home. My parents lived very independent lives, so I learned that if Mom and Dad could go through life blind, what's my excuse?"

Today, Lois is a widely respected journalist and senior writer for the *Deseret News*, the leading daily newspaper in Salt Lake City, Utah. Over a 30-year career, she has experienced all of the turbulence and dislocation of the print journalism world. And like everyone else, she has her own set of real-world challenges, including a husband who is awaiting a liver transplant.

And yet Lois is an engagement outlier. Her patterns of commitment, performance, and adaptability are strikingly different from those of the vast majority of the population. Her work is of exceptional quality, and her productivity is staggering. In her midfifties, she outworks and outproduces cub reporters half her age. "Journalism is a calling," she says. "It's a privilege to tell other people's stories. I give voice to people who don't have voice."

In Lois's case, we suspect that some of her high engagement comes from her socialization. She developed a work ethic and learned self-reliance at a very young age. She also gained a mindset to find joy and gratitude in her work, some of which has grown out of the kind of work she does. "I cover people in crisis and poverty. I tell the stories of the abused and the disabled, and I recognize that I have a really good life."

The question is whether you can become highly engaged without the benefit of such defining experiences. Can you become like Lois without being Lois? That's the question. Dr. Seuss said, "Sometimes the questions are complicated and the answers are simple."

How to become highly engaged is such a question.

The Benevolent Organization

Imagine that you work for the most benevolent organization on earth—an organization that believes in and practices fanatical employee support. The organization has anointed you with a big title, a big office, and a big salary. It assigns people to clean your house, do your laundry, and file your tax returns. There are piano lessons for your kids, personal trainers and home decorators, a pet photo contest every year, unlimited spa treatments, extended family cruises, and ice cream socials. Not least, you have a great boss. In the history of the world, there has never been a more successful organization, and you are exquisitely blessed to be right in the middle of it.

So let's ask: Are you engaged? Are you passionately connected and actively participating in the organization and the work you do? Do you bring your best game to work every day?

Answer: even in these circumstances, you have only a 25 percent chance of being highly engaged.

The organization may lavish you with perks, but those perks don't hold the key to engagement. Feeding the pleasure center of the brain through extrinsic rewards doesn't engage a person and bring real, lasting fulfillment. At best, it creates security and short-term pleasure or hedonic well-being.[1] This is a very different thing from true and sustained engagement.

Happy Dead Weight

Here's a little history lesson. Perhaps you've heard of the "Hawthorne Effect." Professor Elton Mayo did some studies in the 1920s to see what would happen if he changed working conditions in a Western Electric factory outside of Chicago.[2] He turned the lights up in the factory, and worker productivity went up. The employees were more satisfied. At least, that's what a lot of people thought.[3] So for the next several decades, organizations focused on two things—working conditions and employee satisfaction. If we improve working conditions, employees will have higher job satisfaction, and higher job satisfaction will lead to higher productivity. So went the thinking.

The thinking was wrong. Researchers discovered that employees can be satisfied and unproductive at the same time. In other words, it's possible to be content and apathetic—to be "happy dead weight." So they went back to the drawing board. Employee satisfaction was not a good predictor of performance and productivity after all.

In the early 1990s, the concept of employee engagement took center stage. It's like employee satisfaction, but it's more than that. Employee engagement is a cluster variable. It includes several dimensions: how you think, feel, and act. It's a measure of passion, commitment, attachment, and contribution all bundled together. And lo and behold, it predicts productivity and performance and has done so for more than 20 years. For example, the retailer Best Buy can predict with precision that the value of a 0.1 percent increase in employee engagement will translate into more than $100,000 in a store's annual operating income.[4]

Is employee engagement hard to define and measure? Sure it is. But don't get hung up on that.[5] There will never be total consensus on how to measure it, and that's okay. We've landed on a concept that really works, even though there's some variation in the way we measure it.

Most employees are either bored or burned out. We know that because that's what they tell us in survey after survey. Most are disengaged. Even when organizations practice fanatical employee support, they still have huge numbers of disengaged employees. Why? That's what we wanted to know. But instead of asking disengaged employees why they're disengaged, we asked highly engaged employees why they're engaged.

We studied deeply motivated and committed employees across industries, continents, cultures, and demographics. We interviewed them and observed them in all sorts of situations, organizations, and environments. What is absolutely clear is that highly engaged employees think and behave differently. They have a different mindset. They may work in different organizations and do very different jobs, but there's a consistent theme among them: They take primary responsibility for their careers, their success, and their fulfillment. They own their own engagement. They are the driving force. With very few exceptions, they believe that the burden of employee engagement falls on their shoulders, not the organization's.

The highly engaged employees we studied seemed almost puzzled when we asked them why they feel this way. "What's the alternative?" they would ask in response. To rely on the organization, they said, is unrealistic. It might be nice to shift the burden to the organization, and certainly it has a support role to play, but to depend on the organization doesn't make any sense at all. The speed, complexity, and volatility of the twenty-first century make it utterly foolish. That's what they said—again and again.

What startled us was the consistency of this pattern. It cuts across culture, age, industry, gender, and any other demographic you may want to consider. The problem is this: many people don't seem to understand this principle, and we dare say that many do not believe it. In our research, two facts hit us right between the eyes. First, engagement levels are static. In the average organization, only 25 percent of employees are highly engaged.[6] In many cases, engagement levels have actually fallen, and they certainly haven't increased, at least not in the aggregate. Many individuals and organizations have reached the point of diminishing returns; they can't seem to move the engagement needle any further. The second fact is that among employees there is an abundance of what we call an "engage-me mindset." Employees are waiting expectantly for a paternalistic organization to engage them.

We consider this supremely dangerous.

In most cases, the single biggest obstacle to employee engagement is the employee. Employees get in their own way by not taking charge of their professional lives. In the end, it may not matter what we'd like the answer to be to the question: "who owns your engagement?" A globalizing world has given us the answer, whether we like it or not. Tory Johnson of ABC News puts it this way: "If we learned one thing from the job market last year, it's that nobody's coming to take care of our careers. We can't wait for a big bailout, a massive economic turnaround, or some miracle to grow our paychecks. We're each responsible for taking charge and making things happen for ourselves."[7]

As an employee, you have three choices: (1) Accept what you've been given. (2) Change what you've been given. (3) Leave what you've been given. We want to focus on the second option. If you feel underused and undervalued, you can do something about it. You may be tempted to hold the organization accountable for your engagement. If you still don't buy the argument that you're in charge of your own engagement, ask yourself: have you ever had true passion for something in life?

Most likely you can answer yes. So where did that passion come from? You get the point. Nobody can give you passion. Nobody can instill in you deep and rich and vibrant engagement. You have to do it. You should do it.

Engagement drives performance, both personally and organizationally. Torrents of data and reams of analysis have proven a direct relationship between the two. Engagement is the passion you have for what you're doing and the affection you have for the organization and its people. It's the comprehensive expression of your motivation and desire to contribute. Of course engagement levels vary. That's the problem. Some people are on fire. Others are frozen solid. Highly engaged people demonstrate focus, energy, and commitment. Disengaged people languish in complacency, indifference, and halfhearted effort. They think, feel, and act differently from truly engaged human beings. But that's not all. Engaged human beings deliver different results—to themselves and to their organizations.

Individuals who dive in and participate fully earn greater rewards and experience deeper personal and professional fulfillment. Show us a disengaged person, and we will show you lackluster performance, limited personal growth, and diminished rewards. Show us an engaged person, and it's just the opposite—high performance, accelerated personal growth, and inevitable success.

> *"Comparisons between people whose motivation is authentic (literally, self-authored or endorsed) and those who are merely externally controlled for an action typically reveal that the former, relative to the latter, have more interest, excitement, and confidence, which in turn is manifest both as enhanced performance, persistence, and creativity and as heightened vitality, self-esteem, and general well-being. This is so even when the people have the same level of perceived competency or self-efficacy for the activity."[8]*
> Richard M. Ryan and Edward L. Deci, psychologists

There are two requirements for high engagement. First, you have to *want* to be engaged. There has to be a deep-seated desire in your heart and mind to participate, to be involved, and to make a difference. If the desire isn't there, no person or book can plant it within you. That desire is an intensely personal decision. If you have it, you're halfway there.

Second, you have to *know how* to achieve high engagement and sustain it. A lot of people want to be more engaged; they just don't know how to do it. They don't understand the principles and practices behind high engagement. This book can help you with the second requirement. In fact, that's what this book is all about. Our goal is to teach you how to own your own engagement from the inside out.

The Patron Saint of the Disengaged

The comic strip *Dilbert* is published in 2,000 newspapers, in 65 countries, and in 25 languages. The question is why. Why is it so popular? Why does it resonate with people around the globe? Why does it cut through cultural, social, political, and religious boundaries?

Scott Adams, the writer, has an amazing way of poking fun at organizational life. For many, Dilbert is the patron saint of disengaged employees. He's a jaded, sarcastic, cynical employee. Where does that cynicism come from? It comes from the fact that organizational life is often less than we expect and less than it should be. A lot of people find comfort in Dilbert because he gives voice to their frustrations and allows them to laugh and commiserate with a sympathizing, albeit imaginary colleague. We can laugh, but then what?

Research shows that organizations with highly engaged employees outperform rivals in operating income by 19 percent, net income by 14 percent, and earnings per share by 28 percent. And highly engaged employees outperform the moderately engaged by 23 percent and the disengaged by 28 percent.[9] Why does this matter? Jack Welch, former CEO of General Electric, said, "There are only three measurements that tell you nearly everything you need to know about your organization's overall performance: employee engagement, customer satisfaction, and cash flow."[10]

Highly engaged employees get results with energy, passion, and purpose. They engage with customers better, innovate faster, and execute more reliably. Indeed, the highly engaged represent the ultimate competitive weapon. They hold the key to the customer experience. While engagement may have been at one time a soft concept, today it's considered a hard business metric that changes the bottom line.

Why Should You Care?

If you've looked around lately, you'll notice that things aren't the same. The twenty-first century presents us with combinations of speed and complexity that we've never seen before. We call it the new normal because the old normal is gone forever. The old way of doing things is not coming back. For most of us, it has been painful. The consequences of the new normal are reaching down and having an impact not only on organizations, but on individual employees. It's testing our ability to stay engaged.

> *"Our plans miscarry because they have no aim. When a man does not know what harbor he is making for, no wind is the right wind."*
> Seneca the Younger, Roman statesman

The fortunes of organizations rise and fall more quickly in the new normal. The average span of competitive advantage is shorter. You don't know what's coming next. Most organizations are doing their best to be competitive and take care of their employees, but they can't make promises. Who can promise job security? It's simply not something that's within the control of most organizations. Yet it's the highly engaged that have the best claim on job security. Not surprisingly, they are the ones who find the opportunities to grow, develop, and advance.

Outside In or Inside Out?

In spite of all that organizations have done to increase engagement over the last 10 years, and despite all they continue to do, engagement numbers haven't changed significantly around the world. There's a disengagement epidemic across the globe. The data consistently shows that only one in four employees is highly engaged. That's frightening. What about everyone else? They fall into three categories: (1) moderately engaged (just above neutral, meaning neither engaged nor disengaged), (2) disengaged, or (3) highly disengaged. The needle is stuck!

What's getting in the way? Part of the answer lies in understanding what drives engagement in the first place. Two primary types of factors drive engagement: extrinsic factors and intrinsic factors. An extrinsic factor is something that comes from the outside—meaning outside of you. It's something in the environment, something in the conditions or circumstances that surround you that influences you to become more engaged. For example, you may have a great boss, a nice office, or a new computer; the organization may be performing well; or perhaps you've been given a lot of training to do your job and a generous budget to accomplish your priorities. These are all extrinsic factors—things that come from outside. Extrinsic factors are important, and they do have an impact on engagement levels. They create engagement from the outside in.

> *"The greatest discovery of my generation is that a human being can alter his life by altering his attitude of mind."*
>
> William James

Intrinsic factors, on the other hand, come from the inside. They are inherent and are not dependent on outside conditions or circumstances. They are based on what you do. They're based on human action rather than environmental conditions.[11] We've all experienced the power of an intrinsic factor. Just think about the times at work when you felt high motivation or a sense of deep satisfaction. Perhaps you learned something new. Maybe you really delivered on a project. Maybe you overcame a challenge. Maybe you helped someone who needed your help. Maybe you really love the kind of work you're doing. When you notice that your attention and motivation are increasing as you are doing something, that's an indication that something is going on inside, that intrinsic factors are at work and your engagement level is rising. When you act based on intrinsic factors, you don't do it for material or social rewards, you do it for invisible emotional, intellectual, and moral rewards. When you're engaged, it shows. It shows in your concentration, your effort, and your emotion. You can't hide it. Intrinsic factors create engagement from the inside out.

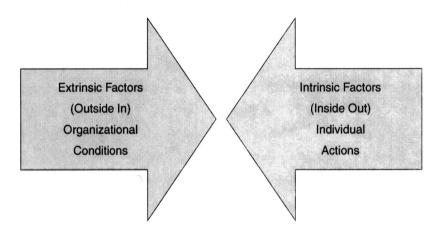

FIGURE 1.1   Extrinsic and Intrinsic Factors of Engagement

- Extrinsic factors drive engagement from the "outside in."
- Intrinsic factors drive engagement from the "inside out."

Both extrinsic and intrinsic factors drive engagement (see Figure 1.1). It's not exclusively one or the other. Here's the point. In most cases, the organization controls most of the extrinsic factors, meaning the conditions in which you work. When it comes to intrinsic factors, it's the individual—it's you—who controls what goes on inside of you. Ultimately, you're the one who decides to be interested in something, to put your effort into something. You're the boss of your effort, your motivation, and your actions. You're in charge of this part of your engagement.

> *"If you're going to be in the room ... be in the room!"*
> Nigel Risner, British writer and speaker

So what do you do as an individual? What do you worry about? Answer: focus on intrinsic factors that drive engagement and let the organization worry about conditions. And guess what? That's exactly what highly engaged employees do.

How Are Highly Engaged Employees Different?

How do you learn engagement from someone who's disengaged? You don't. That's like trying to learn French from a Spanish teacher. People simply can't teach you what they don't know. So we decided that the key to understanding high engagement was to study the highly engaged. We studied 150 highly engaged employees in 13 different industries and 50 different organizations, from aerospace and healthcare to technology and media. Do they behave in consistent ways? The answer is a resounding yes! Here is what we found:

1. **Highly engaged employees take primary responsibility for their own engagement.** When surveyed, 99 percent of highly engaged employees report that they take personal and primary responsibility for their own engagement. It's a stunning and largely ignored fact. The highly engaged expect the organization to play a support role. The highly disengaged expect the organization to play a primary role. While most *highly engaged* employees embrace an employee-centered model of engagement (meaning "I own it; it's up to me; I'm responsible for my own engagement"), most *disengaged* employees follow an employer-centered model (meaning "It's my manager's or the organization's job to keep me engaged"). In sharp contrast, the *highly engaged* don't wait around for the organization to engage them. They take deliberate steps to engage themselves.

2. **Highly engaged employees feel the least entitled.** Highly engaged employees understand they must dynamically manage their employability on an ongoing basis. They are far less predisposed to worry about what the organization owes them. They believe that high performance speaks for itself and that it will be recognized in any setting.

   It's rather stunning, but most of the highly engaged individuals we studied think the concept of a "secure job" is a silly concept. They look at others who believe in such a notion as foolhardy. It's not necessarily that we are going to become a world of temp workers, but a simple acknowledgment that no one and no organization has the power to grant true job security.

3. **Highly engaged employees engage customers.** Highly engaged employees can't help but reveal themselves to customers. They project and infect customers with the contagion of their own engagement. Unfortunately, the opposite is also true of disengaged employees. Ultimately, an organization's brand promise is kept or broken by the employee—the real and ultimate face of the company. Highly engaged employees make the customer experience. Disengaged employees break it. Whatever is inside the employee is sure to come out and influence the customer. Employees always reveal their level of engagement at the customer interface.

"I set myself on fire, and people come to see me burn."
John Wesley, founder of Methodism

4. **Highly engaged employees remain highly engaged almost anywhere.** Highly engaged employees are amazingly agnostic to their organizational environment. We found highly engaged people in all kinds of organizational settings and environments: corporations, governments, hospitals, schools, nonprofits. It didn't matter. They demonstrate agility and adaptability and recognize that organizational conditions are subject to market conditions and the business cycle. Their high engagement is portable; they take it with them. It's both a mindset and a skill set. They create their own weather.

5. **Highly engaged employees apply six behavioral drivers.** Individuals who take personal and primary responsibility for their own engagement consistently apply six behavioral drivers: connecting, shaping, learning, stretching, achieving, and contributing. The ongoing process of applying these drivers allows them to sustain high levels of engagement over time.

Don't misunderstand. We're not saying that leaders and organizations shouldn't help engage their employees. They should! Extrinsic motivators help drive engagement, and leaders play a vital role in fostering conditions that boost engagement, such as creating a dynamic culture, developing good leadership, creating a compelling strategy and vision, aligning reward and recognition systems, and providing ample resources. We are saying, however, that highly engaged employees must take primary responsibility. They must take the lead.

If you put these concepts into diagram form, it looks like Figure 1.2. Organizations are responsible for enabling conditions. As an individual, you're responsible for enabling behavior. If both elements come together, the result is a highly engaged individual. It's important to understand both factors and how they reinforce each other. And it's critical to recognize a significant finding from our research about highly engaged employees: even in poorly performing organizations with lousy work conditions, limited resources, and few opportunities, those who are highly engaged still take responsibility and own their own engagement.

High Engagement = Individual Behavior + Organizational Conditions

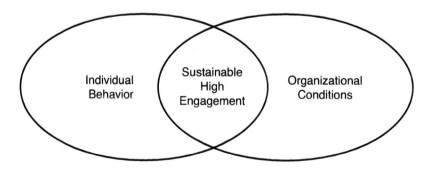

FIGURE 1.2   Responsibilities for Engagement

Here's the principle: Organizational conditions that create extrinsic motivation are important, but never enough. The employee's role is primary. The organization's role is secondary. To maintain high engagement, you've got to take action. You've got to apply the six drivers and create your own engagement.

The Six Drivers of High Engagement

An important and often overlooked aspect of engagement that complicates the issue is that for the first time in our history, we have four generations working side by side: Traditionalists, baby boomers, Generation X, and Millennials. This is important because in their efforts to increase employee engagement, organizations have taken a "one size fits all" approach to generations that can be quite distinct. In reality, a particular engagement strategy might not work to engage both a baby boomer and a Millennial. Many of the solutions proposed for leaders to increase engagement (like Friday barbecues, get-togethers, casual day, or having a best friend at work) don't work across all the generations. Needs and circumstances are different. What is consistent is that highly engaged employees across the board apply the same six drivers, whether you are 62 and close to retirement or 22 and just entering the workforce.

Here's a brief look at each of the six drivers:

1. **Connect: Plug into Your Power!** This driver includes developing great relationships and connecting socially. But it goes far beyond that. There are three other dimensions that are also vital to connecting as a driver. There's an intellectual dimension of connecting, which means that you connect to the work, people, and place on an intellectual level, and you find it stimulating. There's an environmental/cultural dimension of connecting, which means that you connect to the

organization through its culture, its geography, and its environment. And there is an inspirational dimension of connecting, which means that you connect to the organization based on its cause, mission, vision, values, or goals. On this dimension, you connect to what the organization represents and where it's going. To unlock this aspect, you have to discover which of these dimensions help drive your engagement and which one is your primary anchor.

2. **Shape: Make It Your Own!** Although you may not have complete control over your work and your work life, you do have more influence than you may realize. Shaping is the process of customizing, personalizing, and tailoring your professional experience based on your preferences while pursuing the organization's goals and acknowledging real constraints. It doesn't mean that you take a blank canvas and just paint the job of your dreams. Of course not. There are real limits. But it's amazing how many opportunities you have to shape your professional life in three specific areas: your goals, your work, and your work life.

3. **Learn: Move at the Speed of Change!** Think back on a time when you felt the thrill of learning. It was really stimulating, wasn't it? When people successfully learn and apply new knowledge and skills, it fuels their engagement. The highly engaged have a greater appetite for learning. They cultivate aggressive and self-directed learning habits. They're rapid, adaptive, and collaborative in how they go about learning because work environments are in constant flux. Learning at or above the speed of change becomes a personal competitive advantage and a powerful driver of engagement.

4. **Stretch: Go to Your Outer Limits!** Stretching means leaving your comfort zone, passing through your discomfort zone, and pushing on to your outer limits. Stretching increases your capacity to perform. It creates both discomfort and

exhilaration. Whenever you stretch and go to your outer limits, you increase capacity and drive engagement to a high level.

"Far better to dare mighty things, to win glorious triumph, even though checkered by failure, than to take rank with those poor spirits who neither enjoy much nor suffer much, because they live in the gray twilight that knows not victory, nor defeat."

Theodore Roosevelt

5. **Achieve: Jump into the Cycle!** To accomplish is the end result of stretching. Stretching is great, and it builds capacity. But it's not enough. Eventually, you have to get somewhere. You have to achieve something. When you do, the very process of achieving provides its own rewards. Achieving replenishes energy, boosts confidence, deepens fulfillment, and elevates engagement. When you achieve, it becomes a self-reinforcing cycle that allows you to rely less on outside rewards.

"The value of achievement lies in the achieving."

Albert Einstein

6. **Contribute: Get Beyond Yourself!** Contributing is effort directed beyond self. Our research shows that contributing is the ultimate and culminating driver of engagement. Human beings want to make a difference. It's an innate need, and we find that when an individual is contributing to another person, a group, or the greater good, he or she reaches the highest level of engagement. Contributing is the driver that brings the other five together and gives them a higher level of expression and purpose.

"This is the true joy in life—being used for a purpose recognized by yourself as a mighty one; being thoroughly worn out before you are thrown on the scrap heap; being a force of nature instead of a feverish, selfish little clod of ailments and grievances complaining that the world will not devote itself to making you happy."

George Bernard Shaw

Summary

More than anything else, employee engagement comes down to individual responsibility—something that is shockingly absent in the study and practice of employee engagement. There is no aristocracy of engagement. It's not as if some people are genetic or legal heirs to high engagement while others are not. In any field of endeavor, the responsibility for engagement rests first and foremost with the individual. Individualism comes before paternalism. The citizen is primarily responsible for good government, the student for learning, the musician for melody, the sprinter for speed, and the leader for direction. The individual's initiative and effort represent the X factor in the engagement equation.

There's no justification for an employee to wait expectantly for the organization to furnish engagement, as if it's something somebody can give you. You, the individual employee, are ultimately and unalterably the architect of your own engagement. You own it and nobody owes it to you. Engagement is not an entitlement. Nor is it a right. It's a privilege reserved for those who apply the six drivers. It's a choice.

Whether you're the newest member of the shitake mushroom growers association of Australia, chief of surgery at Charité in Berlin, or a microcredit lender in Bangladesh, engagement is an important part of your life. It matters because it is the key to performance, lasting fulfillment, monetary rewards, and overall contribution.

You may work full-time or part-time. You may volunteer, partner, or advise the organization. You may be leading or learning, the CEO or the last person hired, highly paid or a volunteer. Regardless of whether you work in business, government, education, healthcare, nonprofit, or recreation, your level of engagement makes all the difference.

The key to sustainable high engagement is taking primary responsibility for it. Now is the time to own your own engagement. In the following chapters, we're going to share with you what we've learned from highly engaged employees, and we're going to get very practical about it. We're going to show you *how* they do it. It's one thing to read about it; it's quite another to apply it. Our goal is to help you become highly engaged and learn to create your own weather.

Tips for Leaders

Employee engagement is a powerful concept that grew out of traditional employee satisfaction survey research. Over time, it became clear that employee satisfaction, which measures only attitudinal variables, was not always directly correlated with high organizational performance. In other words, it was possible for employees to be satisfied and yet still withhold their commitment and discretionary efforts in work contribution. Eventually, researchers moved beyond the concept of satisfaction. They added variables related to an employee's emotional commitment and attachment and created a broader concept that we now call employee engagement. Because of the multidimensional and more holistic nature of the concept, they have found that employee engagement correlates directly with organizational performance measures. As a concept, engagement is normally considered to include cognitive, emotional/affective, and physical components of an employee's disposition, behavior, and performance.

With the aid of engagement as a concept, and with operationalized definitions that are suitable for measurement, most large organizations now measure engagement levels on a regular basis with employee surveys. In addition, organizations have moved deliberately into the process of creating the enabling conditions that foster higher levels of employee engagement. A focus on creating and strengthening organizational conditions is critical, and if these conditions are designed and executed properly, this may result in a step-change improvement in employee engagement levels.

Organizations following this path often make significant gains, but eventually they reach a point where they can no longer move the engagement needle. We consistently observe that regardless of additional resources and efforts invested to improve organizational conditions and make them conducive to employee engagement, organizations are unable to move beyond their engagement plateau. So what do you do? Here are a few suggestions for you as a leader to help your organization move down the path of instilling an employee engagement mindset in your organization. Our suggestions say nothing about *how* to engage your employees. That comes later. The first order of business is to ask yourself this question: what's your point of view about employee engagement? Until you put a stake in the ground on this issue, we can't talk about how.

☐ Examine and clarify your organization's point of view about employee engagement. Do you have a coherent institutional point of view? Many organizations don't, and that's a big reason employee engagement suffers.

☐ Make a commitment to support employee engagement efforts with the understanding that the employee takes primary responsibility and the organization takes secondary responsibility. If you're not clearly committed to an employee-centered model of employee engagement, you should assume that many of your employees will be waiting around with an "engage me" attitude.

☐ Communicate an employee-centered point of view to your employees clearly and repeatedly so that it's not possible for an employee to misunderstand his or her personal responsibility. This requires absolute clarity about employer and employee roles.

☐ Think about the prevailing culture of your organization. Do you cultivate a climate that draws out the discretionary effort and contribution of your people? Do you nurture a culture of personal opportunity and responsibility?

☐ Can you point to highly engaged individuals in your organization who own their own engagement and sustain that pattern over time? Do you personally model that pattern? If not, are you prepared to start?

2

Connect: Plug into the Power!

"We are caught in an inescapable network of mutuality, tied in a single garment of destiny."

Martin Luther King, Jr.

The Power of Connection

On a spring day in 1978, 15-year-old Britt Berrett was in his backyard. As he had done many times before, he struck a match and leaned down to light the barbecue. That's the last thing he remembers.

A ball of fire engulfed Britt, leaving him severely burned over much of his face, neck, shoulders, and arms. His family rushed him to the burn unit at Harborview Medical Center in Seattle, Washington. The prognosis wasn't good: he would be badly scarred for life.

In the hospital, a team of highly skilled doctors and nurses attended to Britt. He began to heal, but it was a slow, painful process. During those first days in the hospital, Britt developed a special connection with the members of the clinical staff who were caring for him. He could tell the staff had taken a special interest in him. He was deeply touched by the personal and genuine concern they showed.

In fact, it puzzled him. He decided he wanted to do what they did. After two weeks in the hospital, when the pain had finally become bearable, Britt started walking the halls of the hospital burn unit, popping into the patient rooms and introducing himself to other burn victims. After a few days, he had befriended every single patient in the unit. He wanted to comfort and encourage the other patients and their families. As he connected with them, Britt found that he was healing faster himself.

After many weeks of excruciating pain and endless therapy, Britt returned home fully healed. The miracle of it all was that he took with him one small scar on his left arm—a tiny reminder of the terrible accident. More important, through his experience, Britt discovered the power of connecting with other people. Connecting with other patients brought him a sense of satisfaction, purpose, and fulfillment he had never experienced before. Through it he gained a deep and powerful sense of engagement, something that was new to him.

But the story doesn't end there. Britt's hospital stay became a turning point in his life. Before the accident, his family had just moved to Vancouver, British Columbia, and the experience of being uprooted as a teenager was tough on him. Britt felt very much alone at school. When he returned to school after the accident, however, he decided to reach out to the other kids the way he had learned to reach out to the patients. He shifted his focus outward and began connecting with nearly everyone. It soon became a habit. He made it a point to reach out to students who were having a hard time fitting in, those he could tell needed a friend.

The next spring, Britt was voted class president. The following year, he became the student body president of Centralia High School. Britt has moved on to pursue an education and career. Perhaps not surprisingly, Britt is back walking the halls of a hospital, visiting and connecting with patients and clinical staff. He has served as the CEO of three major hospitals in the United States and now runs the Texas Health Presbyterian Hospital in Dallas, Texas.

What makes Britt's story important is that his life could have been different. He didn't have to reach out. Learning to connect and having the motivation to do it was his personal choice. To his credit, he learned at 15 years of age what many adults never learn—that connecting is a fundamental driver of engagement. When we connect with each other—and not merely transact—the impact is felt in both directions.

> *Connecting* is the process of exchanging emotional, social, intellectual, and spiritual value.

In our digital, globalizing world, we talk a lot about connectivity. But that's not what we mean. We're talking about something much deeper, richer, and more meaningful. We're talking about a type of connecting that is unique to our species. It can't be replaced by technology. It's something that the virtual world can support but never duplicate. The multisensory experience of connecting with other human beings, your work, and your surroundings is what makes you singularly human. We strive for it. We thrive on it. When we connect meaningfully, it fuels our engagement. When we don't, we are left hollow, empty, and unfulfilled.

> *"Relationships are all there is. Everything in the universe only exists because it is in relationship to everything else. Nothing exists in isolation. We have to stop pretending we are individuals that can go it alone."*
> Margaret Wheatley, author and educator

Getting a Return on Connection

There's nothing new about connecting. It's a basic human need. We are social creatures who have an innate need to connect. In Maslow's hierarchy of needs, relationship and belonging needs are right next to safety and survival needs. Forming strong bonds and attachments is essential for a healthy, balanced life. It's true for children, and it is no less true for adults.

Here's the challenge: it's pretty rare that you get to live through a major historical shift, but that's what's happening. In the digital age, we have fundamentally changed our connecting behavior. Technology gets both the credit and the blame. First, the blame: unless you live in the Third World, virtually no one lives an unplugged life anymore. Most people are constantly connected, even tethered, to some digital device. The irony is that we can be constantly connected and yet feel disengaged and isolated at the same time.

Many people are confused about how to connect. Society is filled with blanket directives to connect in this way or that. You need this device. You should join this social network. You must have so many contacts. You need to meet so-and-so. You must participate in these activities. You ought to join this organization, take this class, download this smartphone app, or take this survey. It's simply over the top. How do you make sense of this tangle of advice?

Then there's the related topic of networking that's a part of connecting. A lot of the conventional wisdom about networking is flat-out wrong. And it feels wrong because it's manipulative. It's about how to exploit a relationship to get what you want. It says you're not a friend, you're a contact. You're a tool in someone's toolbox. You're a means to someone's end. People are advocating turbocharged methods for networking, and it's all a little much. We don't subscribe to that approach. If you're not a Rolodex Jedi, that's just fine.

When it comes to connecting, we don't pretend we know what's best for you. But we do have a few ideas to consider. In our study of highly engaged employees, we found that connecting is a huge driver of engagement. We also found that highly engaged employees connect in very different ways depending on their personalities, preferences, needs, desires, job requirements, and circumstances. There's absolutely no formula or prescription for connecting.

Don't become discouraged, however; we did find what we believe is the key. Highly engaged employees focus on one thing: they find a meaningful *return on connection*. If connecting is about an exchange of value, highly engaged employees are always asking the question, "Am I getting a high return on connection for my investment?" No one can answer that for you, but you can certainly answer that question for yourself. If you've just spent the last two hours at a networking event and you did nothing but talk about truck pulls and professional wrestling, your return on connection was near zero on a 10-point scale. Move on.

It's a simple metric, but it works. Judge everything you do on the basis of meaningful return on connection. We even suggest that you assign a return on connection (ROC) score to the things you do and the way you spend your time. If your investment of time yields a low ROC—say, something in the 1 to 5 category—cut it loose. At the very least, make some changes to raise your ROC.

Highly engaged employees don't necessarily connect more. They connect more effectively. They are discriminating with their time and invest only in high ROC activities.

Opportunities to connect are opportunities to exchange value. They can take various forms. Some are short; others are long. Some are intimate; others are distant. Some are technology-enabled; others are not. Regardless of the connecting opportunity, you can apply the same analysis. Ultimately, you're the judge. You're trading your time, energy, and resources to connect. What's your expectation? Isn't it to have a meaningful exchange of information, knowledge, motivation, love, encouragement, or some other form of connecting currency?

The danger of the digital age is that we connect and, in so doing, make an investment that brings little or no return on connection. We come away drained, disappointed, or distracted. Not a good exchange. Have you ever traded a half hour of your time to watch an infomercial at 2:00 a.m.? You get the picture.

"I am a part of all that I have met."
Alfred Lord Tennyson

The human need to connect hasn't changed in the digital age. It's just tougher. What we see around us is an epidemic of burnout and boredom. Most people don't connect well. And the speed and complexity of professional life is only accelerating. There are more options to connect, but many of those options yield a low ROC.

Connecting is a powerful source of personal engagement, but you have to do it right. Connecting well is about four things: maximizing your return on connection, avoiding sources of digital addiction and overdose, finding your connecting anchor, and harnessing the power of multiple connections.

1. **Maximize your return on connection (ROC).** Everyone has a need to connect. Making meaningful connections is vital to fulfillment and high engagement. Where are the gaps in your connecting behavior? Do you carefully gauge the quality of your connecting experiences and the exchange of value? How might you change your connecting behavior to get more return on connection?

2. **Avoid digital addiction and overdose.** In the digital age, we're flooded with ways to connect, both to people and to virtual experiences. If we connect unwisely, it can lead to harmful addiction. Knowing yourself and applying discipline and good judgment will help you fight digital addiction and eliminate the potential for overdose. Which connections leave

you feeling depleted? Which connections leave you feeling energized and contributing?

3. **Find your primary anchor.** Most people equate connecting with developing personal relationships. Social connections are a primary and critical element of connecting. But connecting can and does take various forms. In addition to human connection, people connect to other things. They connect to other aspects of professional life, such as the intellectual challenge of the work, the environment and culture of the organization, and the institutional mission and vision. In addition to your interpersonal connections, how do you tend to connect? What is your primary connecting anchor, and how could it be strengthened?

4. **Harness the power of multiple connections.** The highly engaged know how to create a lattice of multiple connections to the people and the organization. When you connect in more than one way, the return on connection is no longer simple addition ($5 + 5 = 10$). Instead, it multiplies the effect ($5 \times 5 = 25$). The impact on engagement increases by an order of magnitude. What are your secondary and tertiary connections? How can you strengthen these to increase your overall level of engagement?

> *"We don't accomplish anything in this world alone...
> and whatever happens is the result of the whole tapestry
> of one's life and all the weavings of individual threads
> from one to another that creates something."*
> Sandra Day O'Connor, former U.S. Supreme Court justice

Digital Addiction and Overdose

Consider the following: the Internet game Battlefield 3 was released on October 25, 2011, in the United States and on October 28, 2011, in the United Kingdom. It's the direct sequel to 2005's Battlefield 2 and the eleventh installment in the Battlefield franchise. Based on manufacturer EA's prior sales information, Battlefield 2 sold more than 2.3 million copies within two weeks of release. Battlefield 3 has apparently smashed that record by selling 5 million copies in its first week of release. EA's statistics reveal that over 2.9 million hours of multiplayer time were racked up during a 24-hour period.

A recent posting on an anonymous gaming blog stated, "I haven't posted much here in the past few weeks. I can't seem to stop playing Battlefield 3. This game is simply amazing and I am completed addicted—so I don't have much time or care to do anything else but play it. I don't eat or sleep or even mow the lawn—I just BF3 all day long."

It's not just gaming that's worrisome. According to a new study from Nielsen, "Our society has gone mad with texting and app downloads."[1] After surveying 3,000 teens, Nielsen reports that the average teenager sends or receives 3,339 texts a month.[2]

Technology is wonderful, but it can get out of hand. When your digital device starts running your life and allocating your time for you, you know there's a problem. When you stop eating, miss work, don't sleep, or seek isolation, you know there's a problem. Connecting compulsively or excessively to a digital device is a very real problem. When it gets to that point, your return on connection goes to a negative value. It becomes harmful to you and to others.

As we become more dependent on technology with our 24-7 connectivity, some people say the need for physical proximity is less. Technology does allow us to connect and collaborate in new ways, but do we really lose the need to be together and connect person to person? Can we replace the need for physical proximity? Never! We need it from the day we're born. One of the most poignant examples of this need is the medical finding that "ensuring skin-to-skin contact with the mom in the first hours of life can cut neonatal mortality by 20 to 40 percent."[3] How much of our lives can we really virtualize?

One study reports, "Being connected around the clock will be the norm in 2020—indeed, it will be a prerequisite for participation in society. Currently, there are 4.6 billion mobile users (67 percent of the world population) and 1.7 billion Internet users globally. By 2020, the number of people using mobile phones will reach 6 billion (nearly 80 percent of the world population) and 4.7 billion people will access the Internet, primarily through their mobile devices."[4]

Are you glued to your gadget? The next time your airplane lands, watch the passengers race for their phones the second the wheels hit the tarmac. You'd think they had been stranded on a desert island for six months. If we're not careful, we can fall into a state of addiction and overdose. Why? Think about it this way: what does it require to watch or listen, or to move your thumbs? Basically nothing. Our digital society requires nothing more than passive consumption. We can be constantly connected and never satisfied.

Picture this: You walk into a restaurant for dinner. After ordering, you notice a family of six seated at a nearby table: mom, dad, and four children, all gathered around the table. What happens next is both humorous and sad. As if it were choreographed in advance, every member of the family grabs his or her mobile device and begins gaming or connecting to the outside world. Not one word is exchanged between family members. When the server comes to the table to take orders, no one even looks up. No dinner conversation, no updates on the day's activities, no warm family interaction—just the sound of six people tapping on their mobile devices. Lots of connection—little connecting.

Where is this going? An Intel Corporation survey found that 50 percent of children ages 8 to 12 have two or more mobile devices, 33 percent of kids would rather give up summer vacation than their mobile device, and 49 percent of kids think it's all right to use a mobile device at the dinner table.[5]

Where Do We Go from Here?

The digitization of society and the increasing virtualization of the organization are not in question. It's happening, and neither you nor we can do anything about it. The way it happens to you personally, however, is up to you. At some point, our digital connections bring diminishing returns. On the other hand, the digital age can bring opportunities to connect in amazing ways with incredibly high returns on connection. For example, a study by MIT management professor Karim Lakhani and Boston Consulting Group consultant Bob Wolf surveyed 684 open-source developers, mostly in North America and Europe. The researchers asked these people why they participated in open-source software programming projects. The survey participants told them "enjoyment-based intrinsic motivation, namely how creative a person feels when working on a project, is the strongest and most pervasive driver." That kind of intrinsic motivation is the most powerful kind there is, and the web can provide that too.[6]

Unfortunately, most of us need to be warned of digital dangers. There are many counterfeit ways to connect in the twenty-first century that steal our time and zap our energy. Take full advantage of the technology that's available, but avoid the patterns of addiction and the possibility of a digital overdose. How do you do this? Step back and reflect on your connecting behavior. For each form of digital connection, what is your return on connection?

> "Systems thinking is a sensibility for the subtle interconnectedness that gives living systems their unique character."
>
> Peter Senge, director, Center for Organizational Learning, MIT

Your Deep Connections

Some connections are so powerful we hang on to them. Others we cut loose. If we're convinced the return on connection is high enough, we stay connected for years and years. If not, we unplug. Some of our connections are deep and significant. They define who we are and what we value in life.

Glenda Shelby grew up in Temple, Texas, during the civil rights movement. It was a difficult time to gain confidence as a person of color, but in Glenda's case, it wasn't the intense struggle it could have been. Some of her deep connections made all the difference.

Glenda's mother was an elementary school teacher who spent her evenings and summers studying for a master's degree, which she earned in 1960. Glenda's upbringing had her working at her grandfather's drive-in and grocery store, singing at the Methodist church, reading in the library on Saturday, or out in the cotton fields with her cousins. With her father working on the railroad, her mother was a fiercely independent woman who taught her daughter four deep connections in life: spirituality, family, education, and Christian values.

When Glenda's mother dropped her off at an all-white junior high school on the first day of school, she told her, "Glenda, if the kids ever mistreat you, you know who you are." That spiritual connection and sense of identity was so strong that Glenda learned at a young age to transcend racial differences and connect to all sorts of people.

Glenda took her mother's advice. She went on to become an executive at IBM, McKesson, JPMorgan Chase, and Accor Hospitality. As she likes to say, "The deep connections of my childhood have never become outdated. They applied immediately and directly the first day I walked into IBM, and they apply today." Over time, Glenda has continued to strengthen those connections. "These four connections define me as a person. How could I give them up? I connect well to organizations and people because I'm grounded in the connections I made as a child. I know who I am. I like who I am."

Like Glenda, if our deep connections continue to produce high ROC, we keep them. If we don't have them in the first place, we're at risk of becoming disengaged. Glenda worries about young employees who sometimes arrive at organizations without deep connections. "The young people want instant coffee. If they truly want to be engaged, they need to slow down a bit and figure out where the coffee beans come from. They need to enjoy the journey and connect along the way."

We also have deep connections on the fun side. They may not offer the same significance in our lives, but they're still important. They help us understand ourselves better. They give us clues about our makeup and the things that bring us joy. Some of life's fun connections include traditions, people, movies, art, food, books, locations, schools, career choices, sports, music, personal interests, values, and religion. The list goes on. So what makes some connections so important and others less so? It goes back to the dividends we receive—the ROC.

I (Mike Baer) think about some of my deep connections. Some of them are a lot of fun, and they continue to provide high returns in my life.

- Family and close friends
- '70s music
- Christmas traditions
- Mountains
- Notre Dame football
- Family reunions
- Comfort food
- Indian Lake
- Classic cars

Some of these connections may seem a little strange to you, but we all have our favorite deep connections, and these are some of mine. As I write this, I'm on an 11-hour flight from London to Los Angeles, listening to some of my favorite music from the '70s. Each of the connections listed above brings back a flood of powerful emotions and feelings that remain with me today. Some of the connections are light and fun. Others are deeper and richer.

'70s music and classic cars! Some of my "light and fun" connections are actually connected to each other—classic cars and '70s music. Back in the day, when I was in high school in the '70s, a few of my close friends had some really cool cars. We'd cruise up and down McKinley Ave. in Mishawaka, Indiana, in my buddy's '69 Camaro with the eight-track blaring. I can remember it like it was yesterday—the blue Camaro with the G60 rear tires, Crager rims, air shocks elevating the back end, cruising "fog lamps" on the front, and the sounds of Bachman-Turner Overdrive pumping through the oversize Pioneer speakers. We'd cruise the strip and then hit the drive-through at Hardee's. To this day I love attending the classic car shows in our town. Some people think they're cheesy, but I've always had huge affection for the muscle cars of the past.

If you jump in my car today, it should come as no surprise that my favorite satellite radio channel preset is '70s music. We'd played it around the house as the kids were growing up and they love it too, or at least they pretend to. The summer after high school, to earn money for college, I got my dream job working as a deejay at a local roller rink, which fulfilled my love affair with the best music in generations.

Could I live without '70s music and American muscle cars? Sure, but these are just two examples of how we connect to some of the lighter and fun things in life that help us stay engaged. But let's go a little deeper with the next example. Let's bring family into the mix.

Notre Dame football, fun in the snow, and comfort food. Being raised in northern Indiana, I learned to love four distinct seasons of the year. The hot, muggy summer, cool, crisp autumn, cold, snowy winter, and welcoming mild spring each had its own significance. I made lasting connections with each season, many of which continue to this day.

I grew up a stone's throw from Notre Dame University, born and raised under the "shadow of the golden dome." Just walking on the ND campus is an experience to be remembered. The Grotto, ND stadium, midnight mass on Christmas Eve, and the lakes and trees are just some of the fond connections I have with the university. Over the past 20 years, ND has become the site of extended family reunions for my clan. Once each year, we choose a Saturday in the fall and we all attend an ND home football game. We gather from several different states to reconnect with one another at a place that is special to all of us. It's not easy to pull it off, but we value the connection and somehow find the time to come to South Bend.

The return on this connection is well worth the investment. We usually get into town on Friday and then meet up on campus at the ND bookstore and head off to the Fighting Irish pep rally. We arrive at Joyce field by 8 a.m. Saturday to get our favorite tailgate spot. We enjoy a solid six hours of great family time reconnecting with one another and dining on our game day version of comfort food (chili, hot dogs, cheeseburgers, potato salad, homemade desserts, and more). The thrill of walking into the stadium with our family and friends, coupled with the anticipation of a victory, is a great feeling. Once the game is over, we immediately begin planning the next year's reunion and get it on everyone's calendar. These reunions include three generations of our family. It's the glue that holds us together and keeps us deeply connected though our family is now spread across several states.

Let me share one more connection. As a kid, when a big snowstorm hit our town, it was simply magical. We'd sled down the hills at Wilson Park, build snow caves in the drifts, and ride behind our pickup truck through the snow-covered neighborhood. One of my favorite memories was taking a night drive on Christmas Eve to look at all the homes decorated for the holidays. Fun in the snow is a deep connection for me. It's one that my wife and I have decided to continue with our own family.

Our children could tell many a story about our Christmas Eve drives and how we pulled them behind the ATV on our snow-covered streets. When our kids come back home for the holidays, they pray for snow and beg me to take them out for some fun. (Though I confess that trying to get the kids to watch some of my favorite classic holiday shows does evoke some yawns.)

But I've also cut some connections. As I think about those, there was a time and a place where the connection made sense, was meaningful, and provided dividends in my life. As time rolled on, for whatever reason, the connection didn't provide a high enough return to me, so I unplugged. Unplugging isn't a bad thing. It simply indicates a low return on the connection and moves us on to other connections that provide a higher return.

Take a moment and explore some of your deep life connections, the ones you've chosen to stay plugged into, as well as some that you've unplugged from, and write your thoughts about them in Table 2.1. The purpose of this exercise is to take a closer look at the enduring value of some of your connections. It's an exercise in self-reflection. In most cases, what you'll likely find is that you stay connected to the things that offer a high ROC. But you'll also see cases where that's not true and you should be asking yourself why you keep the connection.

TABLE 2.1   Deep Connection Assessment

List some of your current deep connections.	Explain why you chose to stay plugged in to each one.	List some previous connections from which you've unplugged.	Explain why you chose to unplug.

Again, what we find is that highly engaged people seldom keep connections that don't offer a high return. There simply isn't the time or resources to invest.

> *"We are more connected than ever before, more able to spread our ideas and beliefs, our anger and fears."*
> Bill Clinton

The Connecting Anchors

To help maximize your return on connection, we'd like to introduce you to four connecting anchors. They represent four primary ways that people connect in the workplace. The four connecting anchors are:

1. Social
2. Intellectual
3. Environmental/cultural
4. Inspirational

As we introduce each anchor, reflect on your own professional experience and consider which anchor might be a primary anchor for you.

The Social Anchor

The social anchor is all about people and the richness of building relationships, working together, and being a part of a team. It's about friendship, teamwork, and collaboration that can last for years. Being anchored socially is about a mutual exchange with people in which you exchange care, concern, motivation, and encouragement. If you're anchored socially, you might say, "I am most satisfied when I'm connecting with people I care about, and they care about me."

Tom Schulte is the executive director at Linked 2 Leadership in Atlanta, Georgia. In 2007, Tom was introduced to a new online professional networking site called LinkedIn. He jumped right in and began to build a personal network of connections. By early 2008, he was well on his way to building a large network of connections, and yet he realized that he was getting very little ROC by simply building a long list of connections. There was no real exchange of value.

He was captured by the topic of leadership and wondered if others would find an open dialogue about the topic helpful, so Tom started a LinkedIn group called Linked 2 Leadership (L2L). His philosophy about how the group would interact was inspired by a quote from a Vietnam veteran and former Hanoi Hilton prisoner of war, Lee Ellis, who said, "Show up as a giver!"

Tom hoped there would be like-minded people who wanted to be givers, but he didn't know for sure. Would there be others with the same attitude and desire to connect on a topic they felt passionately about?

He began by asking the newly formed group, "What's the difference between leaders and managers?" Over the next several weeks, people responded from all over the world, sharing their thoughts. Tom captured them, put them into a set of slides, and posted them on the L2L site for everyone to share. In a very short time, the slides generated more than 100,000 hits. Finding there were thousands of people interested in a meaningful exchange on the topic of leadership, he gathered additional comments and created two more presentations that each got more than 50,000 hits.

Next, Tom started a blog. Soon members of this global group began to reach out to ask if they could contribute leadership content. L2L now has over 180 contributors who have contributed more than 800 leadership articles. What started out as a way to "show up as a giver" has now connected people from all regions of the world. L2L now has nearly 20,000 members.

That all started three years ago. Today, Tom is an editor, publisher, and author. He has gone on to start a popular mega-blog spot called the Leadership Collaboratory that features articles on all aspects of leadership. He has also started the Linked 2 Leadership Blogazine (*blog* + *magazine* = *blogazine*) to more effectively share leadership content.

If you ask Tom where the return on connection lies, he mentions what he calls social shepherding. He believes it's part of his stewardship to help L2L members learn how to create stronger and more meaningful social connections online so they can learn and develop as leaders. The source of his highest return on connection is being able to work with thousands of like-minded individuals throughout the world who show up as givers. Tom maintains that connecting socially is a learned behavior. As we succeed, it creates in us the belief, "I can do this!"

> *"Organizations are no longer built on force. They are increasingly built on trust. ... This presupposes that people understand one another. Taking relationship responsibility is therefore an absolute necessity. It is a duty."*
> Peter Drucker, writer, consultant, and teacher

The Intellectual Anchor

Having an intellectual connecting anchor is not just for those in R&D, engineering, or business analytics. It's for anyone who creates, innovates, or solves complex problems. Those with an intellectual anchor are energized by the rigor and complexity of the work they do. They tend to say, "I'm happiest and most productive when I'm solving, innovating, creating, and tapping into my deepest capabilities."

Kelly Devey is a field diesel mechanic for Rio Tinto, a global mining company. At first blush, this may seem an unlikely place to find a prime example of someone connected intellectually. You might assume that we would profile a scientist. And yet what our research has revealed is that many people are connected to an intellectual anchor in all sorts of unusual jobs.

Kelly spends 12 hours a day driving throughout one of the largest open pit mines in the world, the Kennecott copper mine. The mine is so large that in the winter it can be raining and muddy at the bottom of the mine, and in 20 minutes you can be at the top of the mine, 1,500 feet higher, and find yourself in a raging snowstorm.

Kelly's job is to keep the mine's fleet of 92 large diesel scrapers, loaders, and shovels working. He's a one-man mobile emergency room. If any one of his 92 patients goes down, he rushes to the site and makes repairs on the spot. To give you some perspective on the size of the equipment, the trucks that haul the ore stand 23 feet tall and carry 300 tons of rock in a single load. They are larger than several single-family homes combined and weigh more than a jumbo jet. A single tire costs about $25,000. The giant shovels in the mine scoop as much as 100 tons in a single bite, the equivalent of the weight of 50 cars. The machines move so much earth that after taking his days off, Kelly often returns to find the mine looking absolutely different from what it looked like when he left four days before.

The maintenance truck Kelly drives is a full mechanical shop on wheels, including welders, air compressors, electrical equipment, and a five-ton crane to lift large engines for repair. He explains, "I can do anything out of my truck that can be done in the shop, other than stay warm in the winter."

Why does Kelly love to be out in the pit even in the winter? "I like to think of myself as an MD, or a mechanical doctor; I'm a troubleshooter in the pit. I love to diagnosis a piece of equipment." He adds, "These big machines are very smart; each one is packed with new technology, so they can talk to you." Kelly explains that he can connect into the main computer system of any machine and it will tell him a number of different things about that machine. It can determine whether the injectors aren't firing right, what the current temperature of the transmission is, or how many hours it has been driven in first gear or reverse.

"Even with all of the great technology," Kelly says, "I'm still kind of old school in many ways. I prefer to tap into my experience first. I can often tell what problems a machine is having without hooking into the computer." It takes a lot of patience and analysis because, as he adds, "You know each of these machines has its own personality. Each one behaves differently."

Although Rio Tinto has an outstanding safety record, Kelly says that along with the intellectual challenge of repairing the equipment, he has to "be on" all the time to simply stay alive. Being a diesel mechanic is one of the most dangerous jobs in the mine. Kelly is constantly working around large explosive charges. The other challenge is that the loaders are so large that they can roll over a maintenance truck and not even feel it. He says, "I really like the challenge!"

What is the ROC for Kelly? It's many things, but above all it's the intellectual challenge of problem solving. It's the thrill of keeping these amazing machines operating in the pit. "There's an incredible intellectual challenge to keep this massive operation going."

The Environmental/Cultural Anchor

The environmental or cultural anchor has to do with the tangible and intangible work environment. On the tangible side, it might include such things as having a corner office, a window, a desk, a door, a view, a peaceful environment, open space, or the latest equipment. On the intangible side, it might include the culture of the organization—its people, values, philosophy, and way of doing things. In a virtual setting, it might be the way people talk on the phone and the way they engage and work together. Think about all the ways that people become deeply attached to the environment and culture of their organizations. People anchored this way tend to say, "I'm happiest and most productive if I'm working in the right culture and environment."

Several years ago JetBlue Airways opened a large reservation call center in Salt Lake City, Utah. To accommodate stay-at-home moms who wanted to work part-time, the company set up reservation agents throughout the metro area working from their home offices. On any shift, there are between 200 and 300 agents working the phones, solving travel problems and providing help with flight reservations. The job offers flexible working hours, full health benefits, and free space-available flights anywhere JetBlue flies.

Now meet Brenda Edwards, a JetBlue reservation agent. Why is Brenda so connected to JetBlue? With an environmental/cultural anchor, she values the ability to work from her home office. She doesn't have to commute, and she can create a schedule that is flexible and adapts to her family's needs.

In her initial four-week training, Brenda met 40 new agents, and she built a strong connection with 10 of them. She has taken the initiative to build a virtual community with her colleagues, though each one works from a home office. "We regularly text, e-mail, and call each other during the week to see how things are going. We also collaborate to solve common problems and occasionally trade shifts with each other."

Most of the time, an environmental and cultural connection has a lot to do with physical space and geographical location. But isn't it fascinating that in Brenda's case, her connection to JetBlue's environment and culture is all virtual? She's not in an office, at the airport, or on a plane, and yet she participates in and connects to the culture just as much as the pilot who flies the airplane. Though she works from a home office, the environment and culture of the organization are very real to her. In her case, and for many others working in the digital age, this connection transcends physical space.

The Inspirational Anchor

This anchor fastens people to their organization's mission, goals, or cause. It's the difference the organization makes in the world. People with this anchor believe the organization and the work it does make a difference in people's lives. You've heard it said that people will work for money and die for a cause. That's the kind of people we're talking about. Inspirationally anchored people tend to say, "I'm happiest when I'm serving, caring for others, and making the world a better place!"

Did you know that the U.S. Marine Corps was founded on November 10, 1775? We didn't either, until we met our friend Blaine "Buzz" Butler, a retired Marine fighter pilot. This may be a slight exaggeration, but to Buzz, the birthday of the Marine Corps is a bigger deal than his own birthday.

He explains that most Marines carry with them an emblem of some kind on their person or vehicle to clearly identify themselves as a Marine. Buzz is no different. Emblazoned on the front bumper of his pickup truck, in the place of a state license plate, is the bright red and gold emblem of the U.S. Marine Corps. In his front yard, he hoists the Marine Corps flag on a flagpole. In the mindset of a Marine, you never truly retire: once a Marine, always a Marine.

Why the strong connection? Where does the inspiration come from? He says it comes down to at least three things that all relate back to the institution's cause.

First is the mission. It's quite simple. To a Marine, mission accomplishment is everything. If the mission is not accomplished, everything else is a failure. In the Corps, you're taught not to think about yourself and your own needs, but rather about the needs of your unit and the ultimate goal of completing the stated mission.

Second is qualifying. Because mission accomplishment is so critical, the recruiting standard is very high. "We recruit a very special person," Buzz says. "Not everyone can become a Marine." He adds, "The Marines are the toughest and smartest, and yet we're not looking for the super athlete or the rocket scientist. The recruiters are looking for what we call the 'heart of the Marine.' If you have that, we can do the rest." For Buzz, that idea is summed up in a statement that greets you at the Marine Scout Sniper School in Quantico, Virginia. It reads, "All We Want Is All You Got."

Third, history. From the moment you're accepted into the U.S. Marine Corps, you study Corps history. You learn all about what they call the touchstone battles: Belleau Wood, France, the place where the Marines earned the name "Devil Dogs" during World War I; Iwo Jima; Choson, Korea, and many more. "You learn very early in your service," Buzz points out, "what those who have gone before you have done for you."

We asked Buzz what his return has been on his connection with the Marine Corps. "The Marine Corps is bigger than I am. It's really about the love and respect we have for each other and the sense of purpose we share." After learning about his connection to the Marine Corps, we told him we wished we had been Marines too. His response: "We often say in the Marines that there are only two types of people in the world, those who are Marines and those who wish they were!"

Finding Your Connecting Anchor

As you consider the four connecting anchors, you might be interested to know that most people have one of the four anchors as a primary anchor. Of course, they connect in the other areas, too. We all do, but most of us also tend to lean toward one of the four anchors based on our temperament, disposition, and personality. Now it's your turn. Take a few minutes and assess your primary anchor.

Review the following instructions and complete the exercise in Table 2.2. This is a very insightful activity for many.

1. Of the 16 statements in the table, choose the six that best describe you and your connection to your organization. Put a check mark to the right of the six statements that you choose.

2. Of the six statements that you have selected, cross out the three that describe you the least.
3. Of the three statements that remain, choose the one statement that best describes you and your connection to the organization.

TABLE 2.2   Finding Your Primary Connecting Anchor

The Sixteen "Anchor" Statements	
1. I feel connected to the organization because of my friends and coworkers.	1
2. I feel connected to the organization because of the kind of work I do.	2
3. I feel connected to the organization because it fits my personality and lifestyle.	3
4. I feel connected to the organization because of its mission.	4
5. I feel connected to the organization because of my client, supplier, and vendor relationships.	1
6. I feel connected to the organization because my work allows me to be creative and innovative.	2
7. I feel connected to the organization because of its culture and atmosphere.	3
8. I feel connected to the organization because I feel that I'm contributing to a larger purpose.	4
9. I feel connected to the organization because of my relationship with my boss.	1
10. I feel connected to the organization because my work challenges me and causes me to think and grow in new ways.	2
11. I feel connected to the organization because of the environment and conditions in which I work.	3
12. I feel connected to the organization because of its vision for the future.	4
13. I feel connected to the organization because of my relationship with my team.	1
14. I feel connected to the organization because I have to solve difficult problems.	2
15. I feel connected to the organization because of the security and stability it offers.	3
16. I feel connected to the organization because it makes a difference in people's lives.	4

To get your results, tally up your responses as follows: If you chose a statement with a 1, your primary anchor is social. If you chose a statement with a 2, your primary connecting anchor is intellectual. If you chose a statement with a 3, your primary connecting anchor is environmental/cultural. And if you chose a statement with a 4, your primary connecting anchor is inspirational.

Even before completing the survey, many people think they know their primary anchor. You may also have an anchor that runs a close second. This is your secondary anchor. These anchors may well be the reason you are in your particular line of work or are a part of a particular organization.

Plug into the Power of Multiple Connections

What could be more painful than losing your wallet? Answer: switching your bank. One of the reasons it's so difficult to make the change is because of what the financial services world likes to call stickiness. Here's how stickiness works. When a customer opens a new checking account at a bank, it has gained a new customer. But the connection is not necessarily a strong one. If the customer is receiving only one product or service, such as a checking account, the chances of retaining the customer over the next five to six years is less than 40 percent. But if the customer is persuaded to add just one more service, such as a credit card account or a certificate of deposit, customer retention increases to 70 percent because the bank has become more sticky to the customer. If the customer adds a third product, retention jumps to over 90 percent. With that kind of stickiness, it's too hard to leave because there's a good ROC. The customer has settled into a more intimate relationship with the bank.

What does customer retention in the banking industry have to do with connecting? A lot. The same principle holds true for individuals in organizations. As you connect to the organization and its people in multiple ways, your engagement increases.

Sweaty, Bloody, and Muddy

Not long ago I (Scott Savage) needed some advice on a gift for my outdoor enthusiast son-in-law. Not knowing what to buy, I called the outdoor outfitter Backcountry.com. When most people talk about time periods in organizations, they talk about quarters and years. At Backcountry.com, they think in seasons of the year.

A customer service representative came on the line. The company affectionately calls the reps "gear heads." This particular gear head's name was Kelly. It soon became apparent that Kelly lives for the outdoors. He's an avid snowboarder, mountain biker, and camper, and he loves his job—and wow does it show! Kelly had in-depth knowledge about every piece of gear we discussed, a one-man product tester. He helped me find the perfect gift.

Intrigued with Kelly's enthusiasm and expertise, I asked him about his job. He said he loved working at Backcountry. Initially, he went there because of his environmental/cultural anchor. It was mostly about lifestyle. But that connection has since expanded into multiple connections. He's now getting high return on investment in the other areas as well. He's expanded the breadth and depth of his connection to his work, his colleagues, and the organization. As he likes to put it, "Backcountry is not a place, it's a state of mind, and I work there!"

Notice the different connections that surface in Kelly's comments:

1. "I love being involved in the industry. One of my favorite things is when the manufacturing reps hold clinics for us. We learn about all of the new industry advancements all driving product improvements. Many times we get to try the products ourselves." (Intellectual connection.)
2. "The camaraderie amongst the gear heads is great! Everyone gets each other, because we all do the same things. When it snows 18 inches overnight, we all know what's on everyone's mind.... We can't wait to get out and shred the nar nar. It's a great common bond. As it says on our website, 'No one

thinks it's weird when you show up to work sweaty, bloody, or covered in mud.' We all wish we were covered in mud, too." (Social connection.)

3. "All of this builds in me a strong desire to do better. I am very motivated to give our customers a better experience, to really help them find what they need. I also love to help someone new to whatever sport they are interested in. I get to share my passion and love for the sport and to help them get into the sport in the right way." (Inspirational connection.)

4. "I guess it is easy to sell something when you have our return policy. If the product does not work the way you hoped for any reason, you can return it at any time, and it will be honored. No questions asked. All of us are empowered to make it right for our customers.... it feels like we have the same power as the CEO; it's great!" (Environmental/cultural connection.)

Kelly summarizes his point of view this way: "I would rather make $50,000 a year working at Backcountry.com than $150,000 in a job that didn't allow me to tap into my deepest passions." Keep in mind who's doing the tapping. It's Kelly. He's the one who created a personal culture of curiosity. He's the one who goes through his day asking questions, reaching out to his colleagues, and creating an excellent customer experience. He's created the stickiness and high engagement for his own professional experience.

To Boldly Go

Can you guess the primary connecting anchor of Phillip Meade, the branch chief of the studies and analysis branch, Ground Control Division, at NASA? That's right, it's inspirational. "I think for many of us who work at NASA," Phillip says, "the desire to explore space is something that strikes a chord deep within us. I was enamored with space from an early age and can recall childhood experiences instilling a sense of awe and wonder for space that left an indelible mark on our psyche. Most of us here share a common belief in the benefit that space exploration brings to mankind—not just from the spin-offs, new technologies, and industries that are spawned from the endeavor, but also from the act of exploration itself."

It's not easy to keep the idealism of your youth. Phillip explains that in a techno-political organization, you have to deal with political uncertainty in the short term, so it helps to keep your eye on the mission. You have to stay focused on the aspiration "to boldly go." The inspirational anchor draws the employees' focus above the day-to-day battles and onto the long-term goal, which tends to be much more stable, while reminding them of what it is they are working for. That vision to push out the boundaries of what is possible is what keeps Phillip going. With his desire for growth and discovery, it's his outlet.

There's the inherent compensation that Phillip receives from the work of pursuing the mission—and it is outside of any salary or traditional benefits. There's satisfaction in knowing that the work he's doing is important and can benefit all of humanity. He gets to live out his childhood dream.

There's no doubt that Phillip is inherently wired to connect inspirationally. But it doesn't end there. He's harnessed the power of multiple connections at NASA. Because NASA's mission naturally draws people who are all about mission, Phillip has expanded his inspirational connection to a social connection. He has his own fraternity of mission-driven friends, and the bond they have goes very deep. If you work in a "greater good" organization such as NASA, just a little bit of effort on your part to connect to the people around you pays huge dividends. Phillip will attest to that.

But there's more. Because of the audacious nature of the NASA mission, the inspirational anchor is synergistically related to an intellectual anchor. The work itself is challenging and complex. "There is a literal rush," Phillip explains, "that I have experienced when facing and conquering a challenging technical problem that has never before been faced and conquered."

This rush is accentuated by a belief that the problem being solved is in pursuit of a genuinely important goal. The intellectual and inspirational anchors work in tandem and compound the overall combined effect. What comes out of it all is an incredibly high level of engagement. But it's not the prestige of the job in the eyes of others that matters; it's the importance that you personally assign to the work you do. Phillip confesses, "I have been truly blessed by the amazing experiences I've had in working for NASA, and by the opportunity 'to reach for new heights and reveal the unknown, so that what we do and learn will benefit all humankind.'"[7]

Connecting Power Grid

To harness the power of multiple connections, complete the following three steps and fill out the grid in Table 2.3.

1. On a scale from 1 to 7, where 1 means "not strong at all" and 7 means "extremely strong," rate the strength of your connection today in all four categories.
2. What is your desired return on connection for each category?
3. For each one of the four connecting categories, identify at least one thing you can do to strengthen your connection in that category.

TABLE 2.3   Connecting Power Grid

Connecting Category	Strength of Connection	Desired Strength of Connection	Action to Strengthen
1. Social			
2. Intellectual			
3. Environmental/ Cultural			
4. Inspirational			

Summary

What is it that earns a standing ovation? It's the performer who connects with the audience. What is it that wins an election? It's the candidate who connects with the voters. Is it any different in the workplace? High engagement in professional life is also forged through the bonds of sympathy, the bridges of understanding, and the links of love. Connecting is at the heart of the interdependent human experience. Who can deny that those who connect more deeply are more engaged? The question is what to do about it. There are two basic approaches available to every individual: the organic approach or the deliberate approach.

The organic approach is simply to let connecting happen. It's passive. It's about letting professional life take its natural course, whatever that means. If you take this approach, we hope your expectations are low because your results will be, too. We've carefully watched what happens when people choose to live a professional life in which they allow connections to develop spontaneously based on timing and circumstances. Those who take the organic approach are rarely highly engaged.

There's a better way. The better way is to be deliberate in taking responsibility for your connections. We challenge you to initiate connections that you've never had. We challenge you to strengthen the connections that you already have. We challenge you to extend your reach—to nurture the relationships you have with people, to tap into the cause of the organization, contribute to the culture and environment, and push yourself to meet the intellectual challenges of the work you do. Through intentional connecting behavior, you can choose to create a more satisfying and more engaged professional experience.

Tips for Leaders

Here are a few practical tips for leaders who are trying to help their people apply the connecting driver of engagement.

☐ Take a good look around. When you identify an employee who's not as connected as he or she needs to be, jump in and help.

☐ Have your employees fill in a "Connecting Power Grid" (see Table 2.3). Coach them through the process.

☐ Get to know each employee. Find ways to reach out to each employee in a personal way. If you know something about personality and preferences, it's easy to do. Send her something to read. Write him a specific thank-you for something. Ask targeted questions for feedback on a specific issue. When you take a personal and genuine interest in people, you build connection.

☐ Set the cultural expectation that each individual is expected to reach out. Ask each employee to do something to reach out to another employee. When employees reach out, connections become stronger than when someone reaches out to them.

☐ Ask a less-connected employee to join you in presenting a short training segment at your next team meeting.

☐ Have a coaching session with each employee and seek to understand some of the challenges and rewards related to each person's role in your organization.

☐ Invite each employee to assist you in completing an important task.

☐ Introduce each employee to someone he or she doesn't know but you do.

☐ Discuss the mission, vision, values, and goals of the organization with your employees. Build a shared understanding of these things.

☐ Invite a senior leader to talk to your team about the future direction of the company. Have the leader explain how he or she is inspirationally connected to the organization.

☐ If appropriate, create your own inspirational mission, vision, and goals for your department. Ensure that it's an employee-led process so your people participate and take ownership for the process and result.

☐ When bringing new employees into the organization, assign them to a mentor from your team who is not their supervisor. Have the mentor help the new employee build relationships with other employees. Set specific goals regarding whom the new employee will meet and when. This will accelerate the social connection rather than letting it evolve more slowly.

☐ Facilitate a discussion with your employees that focuses on improving the connections inside and outside your team. Think about the connections that can be made between your team and other teams. Plan and carry out activities to connect to other teams and departments.

☐ Ask your team members for suggested ways to expand and strengthen the environmental and cultural connection they have with the organization and its people. Begin by implementing the no-cost or low-cost suggestions that would make a difference.

3

Shape: Make It Your Own!

"In the long run, we shape our lives and we shape ourselves. The process never ends until we die. And the choices we make are ultimately our own responsibility."
Eleanor Roosevelt

A friend of ours recently purchased a new sports car. After enduring a tedious description of every detail, we asked him how the car handled.

"I don't have it yet," he replied. "I pick it up next week."

Chagrined, we asked, "What? We thought you bought the car last week."

"I did, but it's not ready. It's not *my* car. It's just a factory car. I've got to make it mine."

It turned out that our friend took his new car straight to an aftermarket shop to do a little "shaping." He put on new wheels, new tires, new lights, a new spoiler, a different stereo system, and added some pin-striping and a few other accessories. When he finally picked it up, it was *his* car.

He had shaped it. He put in the extra investment to make it what he wanted.

Now it may not be your thing to accessorize a new car with aftermarket options, but you can appreciate the point. When you shape something, when you customize, personalize, and mold something to fit your personality and preferences, you put yourself into it and create an emotional bond. In some way, it's an extension of you— an investment and a personal commitment. And whether you are conscious of it or not, you expect a payoff. Is it any wonder that shaping boosts engagement? The same principle applies to work and work life—the more you personally shape your professional experience, the more you put your personal imprint on your job, the more that experience becomes uniquely yours.

Our research shows that shaping is a largely forgotten driver in the understanding of human engagement. Highly engaged employees demonstrate a consistent pattern of taking the initiative to shape their professional experiences as much as they can. They understand who they are and tailor the work they do to fit their motivations, strengths, and situation. Fundamentally, they shape three things: (1) their professional goals, (2) their work, and (3) their work life.

A corresponding pattern is that in the "new normal," organizations are more willing to respond to shaping preferences. They're more flexible and more amenable to shaping requests. There are, of course, real constraints and limits. But think about the current environment. Organizations in every sector are motivated to be more responsive to shaping requests. Take Google. Salar Kamangar, CEO of YouTube, one of Google's units, describes the organization this way: "Google has a culture where impatient people can be successful."[1] And guess what? Engaged people are like that. They're impatient because they're passionate. Thankfully, more organizations are getting this. More than at any time in history, organizations are offering you more opportunity to shape your professional experience.

Shaping is the process of customizing, personalizing, and tailoring your professional experience based on your preferences, while pursuing the organization's goals and acknowledging real constraints.

Why We Don't Shape

Alice Walker said, "Look closely at the present you are constructing; it should look like the future you are dreaming." Do you have a future in mind? What does it look like? Is it different from your professional life today? As you look closely at your professional life, it's vital to understand your environment and circumstances. Your expectations must be informed by reality. There's much you can do to move toward the future by constructing a better "now."

Disengaged people feel as if professional life just happens. They often share a victim's mindset at worst or a dutiful, good-soldier mindset at best. They believe they have little influence over their role in the organization. They get stuck, and they stay stuck. It's as if they fall into quicksand and get bogged down. If you ask us, that kind of deterministic thinking is depressing. The two most common traps are dependency and deception:

- **Dependency.** People in this category are on engagement welfare. They feel, think, and act in a way that is self-limiting because they have been socialized to believe that a paternalistic and benevolent organization is supposed to engage them. They cling to ingrained patterns of thinking borrowed from an old industrial age model that believes that the organization knows what is best for each individual and has the primary responsibility to make employees happy. Their handcuffed assumptions keep them docile and passive about shaping their professional lives.
- **Deception.** People in this category embrace unrealistic expectations about the way organizations should behave because they choose not to see themselves and their own performance in the unsparing light of reality. They deny the fundamental principle that opportunity is based on performance. There are, for example, legions of employees across organizations aching for a promotion and wondering why it hasn't come.

Yet they are not willing to look at the image in the mirror to realize that it is their own performance that holds them back. They are like contestants on the television program *American Idol* who walk away stunned after an abysmal performance, never having sought or received candid feedback in front of the judges.

If you want to become highly engaged, you have to think differently. First, grasp your personal concept of career. With that firmly in hand, move forward to shape your professional goals, your work, and your work life. In all of this, we acknowledge limits. You don't have total control over these things, but the new normal is opening the door to greater opportunities to shape than ever before. Every employee has the opportunity, at least to some small degree, to shape his or her professional goals, work, and work life.

The more you shape, the more engaged you will be. Why? Because when you make work the way you want it, you take greater ownership for it. Like our friend's sports car, when you first take a job, it's a factory job. Not that it's bad, it's just off the shelf. It's not customized to meet your needs. Because we have a deep need to control our own destiny, we should take every opportunity to shape our work life.

Many organizations have changed their fundamental approach. They've become more responsive and more flexible than in the past. They recognize that to be competitive, they must attract and retain the very best talent. They know that a highly engaged workforce is the ultimate source of competitive advantage. A major study published by the Society for Human Resource Management concludes that to attract and engage Millennials, in particular, organizations must provide flexibility, understand what types of work and learning experiences they want, and be willing to "customize schedules, work assignments and career paths."[2] An adaptable workforce requires an adaptable organization that understands the need for employees to shape their professional experience.[3]

Many organizations used to impose narrow constraints on what work employees did. They were rigid and unyielding in their requirements for how work got done. They called the shots. Because the notion of paid work was developed within an assembly-line culture, people had to show up at work to be considered working. Organizations demanded that employees be flexible in ways that suited them, and the employee had little room to make counterdemands. For years, organizations have required the labor market to provide different kinds of flexibility:

- Occupational/functional flexibility: The ability to perform different jobs, skills, and tasks
- Geographic flexibility: A willingness and ability to relocate to different locations
- Wage flexibility: A willingness to work for differing levels of compensation based on performance rather than a set wage
- Contractual flexibility: A willingness to work on a per-project, part-time, or nonpermanent basis
- Temporal flexibility: A willingness to work nonstandard hours, including overtime and weekends

These requirements for flexibility haven't necessarily changed, but what has changed is that the requirements are more reciprocal. It's a two-way street. Organizations want you to be happy and productive at work, and they're willing to flex on their end to make that happen. In fact, they're more interested in the value you bring than exactly how you do it.

Today, there's a shift occurring as more organizations recognize the unprecedented mobility of labor and the free agent mindset. Many leaders are more interested in the value employees provide and less in the process of how they provide it. And they are much more apt to respond to proposals about how a person wants to shape his or her professional experience.

"Best Buy Leads the Charge"

Best Buy, a leading U.S.-based electronics supplier, has led the charge in allowing employees to shape their goals, work, and work life. Best Buy is transforming its culture through an endeavor called ROWE, short for "results-only work environment." Employees are allowed to shape how they work, when they work, and where they work, and they are evaluated solely based upon the results they achieve. The intent of the program is to "encourage people to contribute rather than just show up and grind out their days."

The program's creators, Cali Ressler and Jody Thompson, say, "The employer's job is to create very clear goals and expectations for what needs to get done on a daily, weekly, monthly and yearly basis. The simplest definition of a Results Oriented Work Environment [is that] each person is free to do whatever they want, whenever they want, as long as the work gets done. Everything else—when they come in, how much time they spend in their cube, how long their lunch lasts—is no longer [the employer's] concern. The point here is to always redirect focus back to the work." CEO Brad Anderson was quoted as saying, "ROWE was an idea born and nurtured by a handful of passionate employees. It wasn't created as the result of some edict."

Is it working? You be the judge. Those areas of Best Buy where ROWE is implemented have an average of 35 percent higher employee productivity. Employee engagement is up. Orders processed by people not working in the office are up 15 percent over those who are. Among three separate ROWE groups totaling 377 employees, the number who left the company decreased by 90 percent, 52 percent, and 75 percent, respectively, between 2005 and 2007. Because Best Buy estimates the average cost of turnover per employee at $102,000, it is estimated that the total cost savings to the company is approximately $6.7 million.

Best Buy is interested in the overall value employees provide, and employees are responding by shaping how, when, and where they work to deliver that value.[4]

"Hard work is a prison sentence only if it does not mean anything.... If you work hard enough and assert yourself, and use your mind and imagination, you can shape the world to your desires."

Malcolm Gladwell, author and journalist

What's Your Concept of Career?

To shape your professional goals, your work, and your work life, first identify the concept of career that fits you. People have different ways of looking at organizational life and considering what it means to them personally. This is quite a change from the past. If you go back two or three generations, there tended to be just one concept of career—what we called the traditional career model (Figure 3.1). It said that everyone basically moved through three stages during his or her lifetime. Stage 1 was to "learn"—in other words, get your education and training. Learn a skill of some kind so that you can get a job and make a living. Stage 2 was to "earn." Of course that meant to get a job and earn money. Finally, stage 3 was to "burn." The idea here was that you would someday retire from your job, and then you could settle into retirement and burn the resources and savings you had built up over the years.

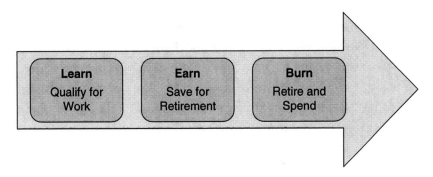

FIGURE 3.1   The Traditional Career Model

That traditional career model is a bit amusing these days, isn't it? It portrays organizational life as a smooth, linear path with clear and distinct stages. Actually, a lot of people did live out their organizational lives that way, and some still do. But most people don't. Most people find organizational life more, shall we say, adventurous these days, filled with changes, surprises, obstacles, and opportunities. For most people, the traditional career model is simply obsolete.[5] The average job cycle is growing shorter and the traditional long job is giving way to a career that is fraught with change and quick turns to the point that the new generation has been referred to as "Generation Flux."[6]

What do we do? Well, we have to find a model that better mirrors both the reality of organizational life and the meaning we attach to it. So what are some other concepts of career? The truth is we've never had so many different concepts of what organizational life is or should be. Some people have a short-term and changing conception of career, so they reach for terms such as a project, a muse, a gig, or a run. Others have the ultimate long-term and permanent perspective and look upon their career as their life's work or their calling.

It's part mindset and part situation. For example, Eric Schmidt, former CEO of Google, explained that a contract worker might see the future in weeks. Others may think until the end of the year when bonuses come out. Politicians see the future as two to four years out based on when their term of office expires. Owners and investors may take a much longer view.[7] Your concept of career has a lot to do with the way you see the future and how far out you cast your gaze. One woman we interviewed likened her career to a water bug—always moving and changing direction. Another called his an expedition. Still another person we talked to thought of his career as a pilgrimage. He wasn't quite sure where he was going, but he felt there was some ultimate destination. Perhaps you know people who look on their careers with the ultimate long-term and permanent perspective. They are the ones who see their careers as a life's work or calling.

A lot of us see our careers as something in between. What about you? It's often true that your concept of career changes depending on where you are in life. Your concept of career today may not be the same as your concept of career tomorrow. There's a good chance that your concept of career is influenced by your generation and the context around you. For example, if you're a member of the Gen Y generation, also known as the Millennial generation, there's a good chance your concept of career may be different from members of the baby-boom generation (see Figure 3.2).

Traditionalists

Born: Between 1922 and 1945 (current age: 66–90)

Total Population: 46 million (in North America)

Percent of Workplace: 5% (in North America)

Primary Trait: Loyalty

Major Influences: New Deal, World War II, rise of the suburbs, Korean War

Broad Attributes: Sacrifice, conservatism, loyalty, discipline, respect for authority, dependable, adhere to rules, duty before fun

Leadership Style: Hierarchy, directive, command and control

Interesting Insights: Often called the Greatest Generation. They put aside their own needs and want to work toward a common goal. They are loyal to institutions such as the church, school, military, or workplace. They have seen the most technology change in their lives: credit card, 1946; color television, 1950; personal computer, 1981; first mobile phone, 1987; Internet, 1991; Google, 1998; Facebook, 2004

Baby Boomers

Born: Between 1946 and 1964 (current age: 47–66)

Total Population: 78 million

Percent of Workplace: 45% (in North America)

Primary Trait: Optimism

Major Influences: Cold War, Watergate, civil rights, Woodstock, JFK assassination

Broad Attributes: Equal rights, ambitious, competitive, idealistic, consumerism, lack of balance, work to live

Leadership Style: Consensus, collegial, best idea wins

Interesting Insights: Sometimes called the Cold War Generation. The rise of television shaped this generation perhaps more than anything else. The personal computer directly impacted their professional lives.

FIGURE 3.2   The Five Generations (Continued)

Generation X

Born: Between 1965 and 1980 (current age: 31–47)

Total Population: 50 million

Percent of Workplace: 40% (in North America)

Primary Trait: Pragmatism

Major Influences: MTV, fall of Berlin wall, 1973 oil crises, space shuttle *Challenger* disaster

Broad Attributes: Confident, free agents, diversity, independent, balance, sense of entitlement, skeptical, informality

Leadership Style: Everyone should be treated in the same way, challenge the status quo, ask why

Interesting Insights: Willing to pursue work/life balance even at an economic cost. Less likely to work for one employer. Seek employer that best fits their culture, lifestyle, and work/life balance needs. Started their careers in period of social and economic change.

Millennials

Born: Between 1981 and 2000 (current age: 11–31)

Total Population: 88 million

Percent of Workplace: 10% (in North America)

Primary Trait: Self-confidence

Major Influences: Columbine shootings, AIDS, 9/11 attacks, election of Barack Obama

Broad Attributes: Civic duty, techno-savvy, tolerance, street smarts, extreme fun, globalism, tenacity, tolerant, entrepreneurial

Leadership Style: Relaxed

Interesting Insights: Most socially conscious generation since the 1960s. Young professionals who are in a hurry for success. Ambitious, demanding, firmly believe they can change the world, have a high need for speed, want freedom in everything they do.

Generation 2020

Born: Between 2001 and present (current age: 0–11)

Total Population: 41 million

Percent of Workplace: TBD

Primary Trait: Immediacy

Major Influences: Social media, Facebook, Iraq/Afghanistan Wars, Great Recession

Broad Attributes: Mobility, media savvy, self-absorbed, life online started in preschool, e-readers, speed, globalization

Leadership Style: TBD

Interesting Insights: Likely to: bring a stronger digital skill set to their jobs than any previous generation; want the freedom to get an education anywhere in the world; assume and demand transparency, access, and speed; drive organizations toward more social responsibility; volunteer more and have more risk tolerance for entrepreneurship.

FIGURE 3.2 **The Five Generations (Continued)**

This is the first time in the history of the world that five distinct generations have worked side by side: the Traditionalists (born 1922–1945), baby boomers (1946–1964), Generation Xers (1965–1980), Millennials (1981–2000), and Generation 2020 (2001 or later). Each generation sees the world differently, works differently, and has different needs. In many ways, the generation you belong to has shaped the way you view work and your professional life. Some see work as a calling, others as a career, and the Millennials often see it as a gig. And what makes this tricky is that even though we work side by side, we all work very differently and shape our world differently. The new generation is already demanding that we allow them to shape what they do at work. One can either accept it or fight it. The best solution is to accept it and to be on the cutting edge by figuring out how to adjust to the new generation of workers. A study by BlessingWhite called "The State of Employee Engagement" found that the youngest members of the workforce—Gen Y or the Millennials—are the least engaged of all age groups: only 20 percent are highly engaged, compared with 26 percent for Gen X, 33 percent for late baby boomers, and 32 percent for early baby boomers. And they are the most disengaged group: 25 percent are disengaged, compared to 20 percent for Gen X, 17 percent for late baby boomers, and 18 percent for early baby boomers. Perhaps not surprising, 43 percent of the Generation Y respondents and 50 percent of the recent hires who are planning their getaway are doing so because they don't like their work. They've discovered a disconnect between their professional life and their concept of career.

> *"Millennials view work as a key part of life, not a separate activity that needs to be 'balanced' by it. For that reason, they place a strong emphasis on finding work that's personally fulfilling. They want work to afford them the opportunity to make new friends, learn new skills, and connect to a larger purpose."*
>
> Jeannie Meister, author

Consider this example. KPMG is working hard to let members of the new generation shape their career:

With his broad networker's smile, stiff white collar and polished onyx cuff links, Joshua Butler has the accoutrements of an accountant. Even so, he looks a little out of place in a KPMG conference room. At 22, he's 6-foot–2 and 230 pounds, with a body made for gladiator movies. A native of suburban Washington, D.C., Butler chose accounting after graduating from Howard University because he wanted "transferable skills." At KPMG he's getting them—and more. The firm has let him arrange his schedule to train for a bodybuilding competition, and he's on its tennis team. Even before that, KPMG got his attention when it agreed to move him to New York, his chosen city. "It made me say, 'You know what? This firm has shown commitment to me. Let me in turn show some commitment to the firm.'" He pauses, a twinkle in his eye, and says, "So this is a merger, if you will—Josh and KPMG."[8]

So what is your concept of a career? To help you answer the question, try the following:

Step 1. Identify a one-word concept of career that best matches you at this stage of your life. If you don't find one that matches you in the list we have provided, think of a different term or description. The value of finding your concept of career is that it helps you clarify in your own mind what organizational life means to you, and it provides a helpful reference for you to consider as you begin shaping. Go ahead and complete step 1 by circling the word in the following list that best matches your concept of your career:

- Amusement
- Art
- Avocation
- Bag
- Biz
- Calling
- Course
- Craft
- Dodge
- Expedition
- Exploration
- Field
- Free agent
- Game
- Gig
- Handicraft
- Job
- Journey
- Lifework
- Livelihood
- Muse
- Necessary evil
- Occupation
- Passion
- Path
- Pilgrimage
- Profession
- Pursuit
- Racket
- Recreation
- Run
- Slog
- Slot
- Specialty
- Thing
- Trade
- Vocation
- Water bug
- Work

Step 2. Write down the reasons you chose this concept of career. Why does it fit you?

Step 3. Discuss your concept of career with someone you trust. Obtain his or her verification of the validity of your self-appraisal.

Step 4. Set a plan for how often you will revisit this concept of your career to check its relevance in your professional development.

Your concept of a career becomes your reference as you begin to shape your goals, your work, and your work life. Keep this in mind as you move forward in all your shaping efforts.

Shape Your Professional Goals

The first shaping skill is the ability to shape your professional goals. Do you have professional goals right now? Are they written down somewhere, and do they align with the organization's goals? Consider this: a clear pattern we found in our research is that people with goals are more highly engaged than people without goals.

> *"You are never too old to set another goal or dream a new dream."*
>
> C. S. Lewis

Did you know that students are now designing their own majors in college if the off-the-shelf majors don't work?

> *More than 900 four-year colleges and universities allow students to develop their own programs of study with an adviser's help, up 5.1 percent from five years ago, based on data from the College Board, a New York-based nonprofit organization of colleges and universities. University officials say at least 70 go a step further by providing programs with faculty advisers, and sometimes specialized courses, to help students develop educational plans tailored to their interests while still meeting school standards. The programs can spark students' enthusiasm for learning and sometimes equip them for complicated, cross-disciplinary jobs or emerging career fields.*[9]

Sound different from your college experience? Maybe. But consider this: "Some 27 percent of workers who graduated from college 10 or more years ago still haven't found a job related to their college major; 12 percent said it took five years or more to find a job in their field and 21 percent said it took three years, says a recent survey of 2,042 college-educated workers."[10] Anya Kamenetz, author of *DIY U*, a new book critical of higher education, summarizes the trend best by saying that the concept "introduces the idea that students should be in charge of designing their own learning plans."[11]

Of course, there is a spectrum when it comes to shaping your professional goals—from no shaping to radical shaping. For example, we met a man once who announced that he didn't believe in goals, that you should simply let life happen to you, and that any attempt to plan anything or set any goals was contrary to fate and the order of the universe. We don't recommend this approach. As John Lennon said, "Life is what happens to you when you're making other plans." If you get bumped out of your plans, fine. But make the plans and set the goals anyway, because it's also true that much can and does go according to plan.

On the other hand, there's another extreme. We met a woman who had set a whole series of organizational goals and had planned out her career to the day of retirement. She was going to do this and do that, accomplish this and accomplish that, all based on predetermined dates and plans. Her organization and ability to plan were admirable, but professional life isn't that neat, tidy, or controllable. So we don't suggest that approach, either. What we do suggest is that you take a practical and commonsense approach and establish some goals to increase your engagement. From a professional development standpoint, that's manageable, but if you go beyond that and set all kinds of goals, what happens? The answer is, not a lot.

> *"He who has a why to live can bear with almost any how."*
> Nietzsche

Here are some steps to follow as you set your professional goals:

Step 1. Identify what matters most to the organization. Test your assumptions with others in the organization.

Step 2. Identify what you want to accomplish. Define the impact you want to have and write it down.

Step 3. Connect what you want to accomplish with the organization's goals.

Step 4. Set your personal goals accordingly, ensuring that the objectives you choose are clearly aligned with the objectives of the company. Never work at cross-purposes. Tight alignment with your boss's and organization's goals contributes to greater trust, freedom, and empowerment. Remember, don't set too many goals. Focus on a few things you know you can accomplish that will have high impact to the organization and be personally rewarding and engaging.

Step 5. Once you have identified your goals, use these four questions to set your plan to accomplish them:

- **What are the opportunities, resources, and constraints for achieving the goal?** Think this through carefully. You need to take advantage of opportunities and resources, and yet acknowledge constraints, or you're not being realistic, and you probably won't achieve your goal.
- **What is your time frame for achieving the goal?** Is it reasonable? Is it attainable? Have you put it into your calendar?
- **What is your plan to achieve the goal?** It's hard to tell you exactly how much to plan. You have to use your judgment so that you're not underplanning or overplanning. And you have to be willing to be flexible and change your plans. But in general, what are the four or five actions you could take to achieve your goal?
- **How will you hold yourself accountable to achieve the goal?** This is the challenge with personal goals—there is rarely any kind of accountability mechanism. So think this through. Just writing your goals down creates some accountability. If you tell another person, you create more accountability. If you set a deadline, you create even more accountability. If you invest resources of any kind toward your goal, that also tends to add accountability. Remember, you own it, so build some accountability into it.

One study found that "engaged employees are not just committed. They are not just passionate or proud. They have a line-of-sight to their future and to the organization's mission and goals."[12] The highly engaged understand the ultimate purpose of their role, the contribution they are expected to make, and how they personally connect to the organization's mission, vision, strategy, and goals.

Companies like Genentech, Georgetown University Hospital in Washington, D.C., and Hermann Miller, the American furniture maker, have employees shaping their work by allocating large chunks of discretionary time to pursue projects of their own choosing—areas that line up with their interests. And what's the impact? Joyce Gioia believes that when workers are free to undertake creative ventures, they become more devoted to their jobs and employers at a time when loyalty is becoming precious. Holly Butler, senior staffing manager for Genentech's research group, said, "Discretionary time is a huge piece of why they want to work at Genentech. It is Disneyland for scientists."[13]

Your personal connection to the organization's mission, vision, strategy, and goals is based on the degree to which those things match your personal aspirations, talents, and interests. Figure 3.3 shows the four professional goal quadrants. Try to focus your shaping goals in the upper right quadrant (high personal and organizational benefits) and stay away from the lower left (low personal and organizational benefits). You may find times when your organization needs you to participate in the lower right (low personal benefits but high organizational benefits); this you should always do.

Here's a suggestion. Answer the questions in Table 3.1 for each professional goal you set. After completing the exercise, you may discover that your goals more closely align with a different job within (or outside) of the organization. That's good information because it could lead you to look at a different role that more closely aligns your goals with the organization's goals. Recent best practice indicates that such a move doesn't have to be a promotion. A lateral move, if done right, no longer puts you at risk of

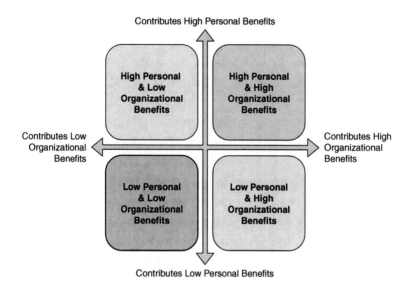

FIGURE 3.3   The Four Professional Goal Quadrants

TABLE 3.1   Your Professional Goals

Goal Questions	Goal Answers
1. How does the personal goal align with the organization's goals? How does it contribute to the organization's strategic goals?	
2. What are the opportunities, resources, and constraints that affect achieving the personal goal?	
3. What is your time frame for achieving the personal goal?	
4. What is your plan to achieve the personal goal? What are the concrete steps you have in mind for making it happen?	
5. How will you hold yourself accountable to achieve your personal goal?	

hitting a dead end. As Joanne Cleaver argues, there are smart lateral moves. "Over is the new up," she says. Cox Communications has gone so far as to view lateral moves as developmental opportunities rather than as what has previously been viewed as a parking spot. And some companies like Deloitte have popularized the idea of a "career lattice" rather than a "career ladder"—an idea that illustrates how your goals might be better met by moving sideways or diagonally versus only in up-or-down directions.[14]

Shape Your Work

Your second shaping skill is to shape your work. Many organizations benefit from employees shaping their own work. For example, two Australians, Scott Farquhar and Mike Cannon-Brookes, founded Atlassian in 2002. They wanted to spark greater creativity and enable their computer programmers to have fun at work. They encouraged their employees to spend a day working on any problem they wanted—even if it wasn't part of their regular job. The result was new products and plenty of repairs and patches on existing ones. The program was so successful that it became part of the permanent culture at Atlassian. At one point, the founders called these "FedEx Days" because people had to deliver something overnight—within a 24-hour period. One engineer said, "Some of the coolest stuff we have in our products today has come from FedEx Days." The founders believe, "Money is only something you can lose on. If you don't pay enough, you can lose people. But beyond that, money is not a motivator. What matters are these other features."

Today, Atlassian developers spend 20 percent of their time—rather than just one intense day—working on any project they want. In one year alone, the company launched 48 new products. Cannon-Brookes says that when the financial guy pushes him on productivity, "I show him a long list of things we've delivered. I show him that we have zero turnover in engineering. And I show him that we have highly motivated engineers who are always trying to perfect and improve our product."[15]

One of the most well-known examples of a company benefiting from employees shaping a part of their work is the American company 3M. Technical staff members spend up to 15 percent of their time on projects of their choosing. Post-it Notes is probably the most famous example resulting from this free time. Scientist Art Fry was annoyed that he didn't have a good solution for paper bookmarks in his church choir hymnal. Piggybacking on fellow researcher Spencer Silver's discovery of a "low tack" adhesive five years earlier, Fry came up with his idea for the "sticky note" during his 15 percent time. Despite its first-year failure (due to customers not knowing they had a need), Post-its are today a huge business with hundreds of different products all over the world.

Many of us today are the beneficiaries of Google products created by employees who shape the work they do. At Google, engineers spend one day a week working on projects that aren't necessarily in their job descriptions. They use this time to develop something new or, if they see something that's broken, to fix it. Half of Google's products have come out of this 20 percent time, including Gmail, Google News, Orkut social networking software, Google Talk instant message application, Google Sky (which allows astronomically inclined users to browse pictures of the universe), Google Translate translation software for mobile devices, and Google Moderator (an application that allows participants to vote on which submitted question they want answered).[16]

Consider the actual work you do in your current job. To shape your work, you have to know two things. First, what kind of work engages you the most? And second, are there any opportunities for you to do more of that kind of work?

There's a concept called *flow*, originally named by Mihaly Csikszentmihalyi, a renowned psychologist from the University of Chicago. *Flow* refers to "a state of being fully absorbed and energized in an activity." When you're in a state of flow, "goals are very clear, feedback is immediate, there is a relationship between what a person has to do versus could do. The challenge isn't too easy nor is it too difficult. It is a notch or two beyond current abilities, which stretches the body and mind in a way that makes the effort itself the most delicious reward."[17]

Sound squishy or soft? Look at these results. A number of companies, including Microsoft, Patagonia, and Toyota, have realized that creating flow-friendly environments helps people increase productivity and satisfaction.[18] Another study surveyed 684 open-source developers, mostly in North America and Europe, asking them why they participated in open-source projects. They found "that enjoyment-based intrinsic motivation, namely how creative a person feels when working on a project, is the strongest and most pervasive driver."[19] They were in a flow state.

Almost all of us at some time or another have experienced a flow state. You can tell when it happens because you're in the groove and you tend to lose track of time.

> *"I believe no one can afford, endure, or can stomach leaving half a life in the parking lot when she or he goes to work. It's a lousy way to live and a lousy way to work."*
>
> Ricardo Semler, CEO of Semco Group

We have a good friend who is a hand surgeon. When anyone in the area has a serious hand injury, he or she comes to see our friend, Dr. Mark Sanderson. One day, we asked him how his day had gone. He said he'd been up all night reattaching someone's severed fingers. The surgery had taken 10 hours. Surprised, we asked if he got sleepy or tired during the surgery. He said, "Never." In fact, "during the long surgeries, I'm in my element. I go into the zone. By the time I'm done, I'm exhausted, but I'm absorbed and focused during the surgery." Now that's a great example of flow. Of course, we can't always be in a flow state. In fact, most of us have to do a lot of things in our jobs that we don't like. That's part of life. But when you do experience flow, pay attention. Gather clues about what kind of work lights you up. What work puts you in the zone? What factors contributed to this flow-state experience? What was the actual work you were doing, and what were the conditions around you? What allowed you to have this experience?

Table 3.2 shows an activity to help you start shaping your work. For each of the dimensions of work, place a dot on the continuum that best represents your work preference. Then connect the dots to see the trend line of your work preferences.

Other things to consider include working internationally, working with virtual teams, and working day shifts or night shifts. The combinations are countless. Think through what your preferences are. Then, based on everything that you have been able to learn about the kind of work you are drawn to and what your work preferences are, use Table 3.3 to write down some opportunities you might have to shape your current work.

TABLE 3.2   Work Preference Assessment

Strategic	◄ - - - - - - - - - - - - - - - - - - - ►	Tactical
Ideas	◄ - - - - - - - - - - - - - - - - - - - ►	Things
Large groups	◄ - - - - - - - - - - - - - - - - - - - ►	Small groups
Creative	◄ - - - - - - - - - - - - - - - - - - - ►	Operational
Nontechnical	◄ - - - - - - - - - - - - - - - - - - - ►	Technical
Experimental	◄ - - - - - - - - - - - - - - - - - - - ►	Routine
Program	◄ - - - - - - - - - - - - - - - - - - - ►	Project
Collaborative	◄ - - - - - - - - - - - - - - - - - - - ►	Individual
Interpersonal	◄ - - - - - - - - - - - - - - - - - - - ►	Solo
High risk	◄ - - - - - - - - - - - - - - - - - - - ►	Low risk
Self-directed	◄ - - - - - - - - - - - - - - - - - - - ►	Other-directed

TABLE 3.3   Opportunities to Shape Your Current Work

Work Preference 1:	Opportunity:
Work Preference 2:	Opportunity:
Work Preference 3:	Opportunity:

A human resources manager completed this exercise and identified a work preference for doing project work. Specifically, she realized that she had enjoyed working on big events during the past year. As a result, she asked her supervisor if there would be a chance for her to do more event planning in her current role. Her supervisor immediately adjusted some of her responsibilities and put her in charge of the company's next major employee conference.

Work should be rewarding and engaging. Attending school teaches us that there are subjects we intuitively love and there are subjects that we find of little interest. Finding work in your organization that you truly love and aligning yourself to that work will create increased job satisfaction and a desire to do your best.

Stanford Business professor Jeffrey Pfeiffer said, "People are looking for the opportunity to have variety in their work and to tackle challenging assignments."[20] Once you get a firm grasp on the unique value that you can offer in the value chain of the organization's mission and the strategic goals it is trying to accomplish, you will more likely expend your discretionary effort to make a difference and get results. As one author put it, "If work is inherently enjoyable, then the external inducements [that] are the heart of [traditional] motivation [become] less necessary."[21]

> *"Work is about a search for daily meaning as well as daily bread, for recognition as well as cash, for astonishment rather than torpor; in short, for a sort of life, rather than a Monday-Friday sort of dying."*
>
> Studs Terkel

Study after study shows that rewarding work is a far more powerful motivator than incentive systems. In fact, an April 2002 poll of thousands of working and nonworking individuals conducted by Monster.com, a website for job seekers, found that

73 percent of respondents said they would accept less money if they could be happier at work.[22] Think about a time when you received a raise. You were pumped, ready to work long hours to show loyalty to the company. But how long did that feeling last? Usually only a short time after you began to spend the new money. Then things went back to normal. It is not monetary systems, but compelling and satisfying work that has lasting power.

Too often we meet with executives who are either burned out, rusted out, or want out. In short, they have "retired on the job." Somehow these leaders have become disconnected with the intrinsic motivators in their work that in the past kept them excited and engaged. Or they haven't stepped forward to match their intrinsic motivators with the work they do day in and day out.

Frederick Herzberg, the father of motivational theory, said, "I can charge a person's battery, and then recharge it and recharge it again. But it is only when one has a generator of one's own that we can talk about motivation. One then needs no outside stimulation. One wants to do it."[23] Shaping one's work involves finding those intrinsic motivators that, like the generator, keep people engaged in what they do.

> *"Addressing this human longing—shaping organizational identity and maintaining consistency between work and personal values—is the key to creating discretionary energy and is therefore a key leadership skill today."*
> Tamara J. Erickson, author

Remember, shaping your work isn't a onetime thing. Periodically, take the opportunity to understand what creates a flow state for you. Assess how well the work you are doing matches your work preferences. Look for those intrinsic motivators. Finally, look for opportunities to shape your work.

Shape Your Work Life

In addition to shaping goals and shaping work, individuals must shape the conditions in which they work. We call this shaping your work life. Most people place a high value on the ability to have control and flexibility in their work lives. Working under confining conditions, as defined by the employee, works against high engagement.

> *"Nothing is more important to my success than controlling my schedule. I'm most creative from 5 to 9 a.m. If I had a boss or co-workers, they would ruin my best hours one way or another."*
>
> Scott Adams, Dilbert creator

Shaping your work life is about shaping the climate, culture, and conditions of your working environment. A survey by the research firm Robert Half International found that "one-third of all executives surveyed have changed their opinions in the last few years, and now say that the work environment is the most critical factor in keeping an employee satisfied in today's business world."[24] In the global age, organizations give more room than ever in allowing individuals to be the designers of their own work life.

Consider that in 2006, of the "100 Best" places to work, 79 allowed employees to telecommute regularly. In 1999, only 18 of the "100 Best" allowed employees that option. At Republic Bancorp, for example, a full 60 percent of employees work from home. *Fortune* magazine's study also found that 81 companies offer compressed workweeks, consisting of 10- and 12-hour shifts. That's a huge jump from 1999, when only 25 companies offered employees that option. In the United States, 33.7 million people telecommute at least one day a month, and 14.7 million do so every day, placing a lot of workers in a position to shape their own work.[25]

"Choose a job you love, and you'll never have to work a day in your life."

Confucius

Sadly, not all organizations are so enlightened. But they end up paying a heavy price for their inflexibility. A large Fortune 500 company we work with has been investing in mobile workstations to reduce the footprint of required office space and provide flexibility in how and where people work. And yet we were on-site when the CEO sent out a memo saying in essence, "We want you mobile. We want you with our customers... and we want you in the office every day because we're worried that many of you are taking advantage of the flexibility and aren't really working." This was likely a knee-jerk reaction—an old-school mentality that believes work happens in the office and is best measured by the number of cars in the parking lot. Sadly, the CEO didn't understand what William McKnight, 3M's president and chairman, said back in 1948, "Hire good people and leave them alone." He went on to say, "Those men and women to whom we delegate authority and responsibility, if they are good people, are going to want to do their jobs in their own way."[26] The new normal is that work happens whenever and wherever it needs to. Regrettably, one employee at our client later told us, "I was working extra hours and on weekends. But if they don't trust me and that's the way it's going to be, then I'll go back to my standard work schedule." Another told us, "That was the nail in the coffin—that's when I decided it was time to start looking for another job outside the company." What a lost opportunity to engage the workforce.

Fortunately, our client example is not the trend. On the contrary, many organizations are engaging in conversations that facilitate employees shaping the way they work. At IBM, for example, a thousand software developers working in different time zones have been given the flexibility to decide when they work. Many of the developers have also chosen to split their workdays into smaller chunks, taking time off intermittently through their days to deal with other aspects of their lives. The time it takes to update a given software product has been reduced from 18 to 24 months five years ago to 4 to 6 months today. As Patty Dudek, an IBM vice president, put it, "If we want top talent to work on something and we give them all the flexibility they need to balance their lives, then they're more than willing to step up to the challenge when we need them to drop everything."[27]

> *"A great deal of employee satisfaction occurs when individuals have some leverage over the logistics of their job."*
> Ricardo Semler, CEO of Semco Group

At Chubb Insurance, a group of employees was given the opportunity to choose the work hours that best suited them. Some 400 have participated so far, and in the Chicago office nearly 75 percent of the employees—120 of the 163—work nonstandard schedules they've created. Their productivity gains have been striking: an increase from 82 percent to 91 percent in customers being contacted within 24 hours, and from 90 percent to 100 percent in timely benefit payments to claimants. "It's making people more responsible and accountable for what they do," says John Finnegan, Chubb's CEO. "The test is that they can do it better than they've done it before."[28]

Clearly, there is a shift toward employees shaping and designing their workweek and work environment in a way that is a win-win for both the individual and the organization. Why? Because great organizations go to great lengths to be responsive to highly engaged employees who treasure the freedom to do their job as they think best—in other words, to employees seeking to shape their work life. When they do this, they release their creative potential and more fully contribute to the success of the organization.

In order to drive your own engagement through shaping your work life, you must first assess the conditions under which you do your best work. Questions to ask include, What conditions have helped produce great work in the past? When have I had a career-best experience? What created that? How do I like to work physically and socially?

> *"Our moral responsibility is not to stop the future, but to shape it. To channel our destiny in humane directions and to ease the trauma of transition."*
> Alvin Toffler

To shape your work life, think about four specific things:

- **First,** *where* **you work.** Go from big to small as you think about this. Do you like where you are geographically? Do you like your work location? Do you like your office or your workstation? Do you like the setting, the atmosphere, the environment, the culture? What would you like to change? What do you need to change? A senior IBM officer shared that at any point in time, 40 percent of IBM employees are working at a customer site, at home, or at conferences. Would that work for you? What would work better than what you are doing now?
- **Second,** *when* **you work.** Do you work a traditional or nontraditional schedule? Do you work full-time or part-time? Is your schedule rigid? Do you have flexibility? What would you like to change? What do you need to change? Time has become a scarce resource and in a way the most valued asset.
- **Third,** *with whom* **you work.** Do you work with people? How many? How often? Do you like the people you work with? Do you like your colleagues, your boss, your customers, your partners? Why or why not? What would you like to change? What do you need to change? The Gallup organization claims that having a best friend at work increases engagement. That might or might not be the case for you.

Gallup also says that most employees leave an organization because of their boss, not because of the company. We're not saying to leave if you don't like your boss. But we are saying to work on improving your relationships and, as they get better, your engagement will increase. (We talk more about this in Chapter 2.)

- **Fourth,** *how* **you work.** We covered some of this in our discussion about shaping the actual work you do. But let's take it a step further. How do you do your work? Are you closely or loosely managed? Do you have a little or a lot of independence? What are your role and your responsibilities? What are the tasks you're responsible for? Do you get enough direction and guidance? If you could, what would you change about the way you currently work? What do you need to change about the way you currently work? In an increasingly busy world with unlimited demands on our time, being able to determine how one works is becoming a bargaining chip between employee and employer.

Research shows that the more you can shape your work life to better fit your needs, desires, and preferences, the more engaged you will be. So here's an exercise to help you begin shaping your work life. Follow these six steps to fill out Table 3.4.

Step 1. Consider *where* you work. What preferences do you have when it comes to where you work? Fill in the boxes in the first row of the table.

Step 2. Consider *when* you work. What preferences do you have when it comes to when you work? Fill in the boxes in the second row of the table.

Step 3. Consider the people you *work with*. What preferences do you have when it comes to the people with whom you work? Fill in the boxes in the third row of the table.

TABLE 3.4   Dimensions of Work Life Preferences

Dimension	Preferences	Constraints
Where you work.		
When you work.		
With whom you work.		
How you work.		

Step 4. Consider *how* you work. What preferences do you have when it comes to how you work? Fill in the boxes in the fourth row of the table.

Step 5. Once you have identified your preferences related to where, when, with whom, and how you work, go back and identify any organizational constraints you know about. Then eliminate anything that's unrealistic.

Step 6. Finally, rank your preferences in the order of their importance to you.

Shaping your work life increases your engagement. Don't let the fact that few others may be shaping their work lives deter you from shaping yours.

> *"People continue to assume that chaos would ensue if everyone were left to choose their own work time. Journalists tell me that newspapers wouldn't be published some days, doctors say that operations would be canceled due to an anesthetist who didn't show up, actors insist that their play's curtain wouldn't rise, and transport specialists maintain that the subway would shut down. Nonsense. What a disheartening view of humankind."*
>
> Ricardo Semler, CEO of Semco Group

Have a Shaping Discussion

There certainly are constraints and limits to shaping. But more often there are opportunities that are simply missed because an employee doesn't look into something, doesn't ask, and doesn't present the organization with the idea or proposal about how a shaping request might be of mutual benefit to the organization and the employee. Don't do this to yourself or your organization. Avoid the quicksand. Resolve to shape your professional goals, your work, and your work life.

> *"What you don't ask for stays the same."*
> Beverly L. Kaye, author

After you have worked through the exercises in this chapter and thought through your options, what and how you shape will come down to having a shaping discussion with your supervisor. This is where you will present him or her with your shaping solutions and ask for support. Think back over the chapter and take a minute to prepare for that conversation. It's important to prioritize your preferences. Ask yourself these questions: What are the benefits that meeting my prioritized preferences will bring to the organization? What's the business case for why I want to change? Do my proposed solutions align with the strategy and goals of the organization? What potential objections might be raised, and how might I respond?

Here's an activity that can help you prepare for your shaping discussion. Use Table 3.5 to record your responses to the following steps:

Step 1. Pick out your prioritized preferences from the previous shaping activities.

Step 2. Write down the benefits that meeting your preferences will bring to the organization.

TABLE 3.5　Preparation for a Shaping Discussion

Prioritized Preferences	Benefits to the Organization	Potential Objections	Solutions to Potential Objections

Step 3. Identify potential objections that might be raised against your prioritized list.

Step 4. Identify your solutions to potential objections.

Keep in mind the following guidelines as you prepare for your shaping conversation.

- Practice before you go.
- Begin by stating what's going well.
- State what you would like to shape.
- Explain the benefits to the organization.
- Address any concerns.
- Demonstrate good faith.
- Seek mutual benefit.

When you have a shaping conversation with your boss, there's a chance that he or she will respond "no" to your suggestions. Some jobs allow more flexibility and room to shape than others. Your own performance, credibility, and tenure will help you gain support for your shaping request. If you're new in the organization, or if your current results aren't what they need to be, don't run off and make a bunch of shaping requests. Assess your credentials (be realistic), summarize your results and the positive impact to the organization, and then be creative in your thinking. If your analysis shows you that you're not ready to shape everything, find something small that you can shape—anything to make your work more your own. And then if you get a "no" response, we suggest you listen carefully to the reasons for the "no." And then do one of five things:

1. Ask again (in a different way or at a different time).
2. Ask how you can help make it work (brainstorm possibilities).
3. Ask someone else (can someone else help you with your request?).
4. Ask what's possible, if not what you are proposing.
5. Ask what you can do to improve the way you're asking. Don't give up.[29]

Conclusion

A Boston Consulting Group study found that 85 percent of executives expect a big rise in the number of "unleashed" workers over the next five years. At IBM, 40 percent of the workforce doesn't have an official office. Sun Microsystems estimates it has saved $400 million in real estate costs over six years by allowing nearly half of all employees to work anywhere they want. What does it all mean? Shaping is a critical driver for the future success of organizations and employees. Great organizations go to great lengths to be responsive to highly engaged employees who value the chance to customize their professional experience.

> *"It is never too late to be what you might have been."*
> George Eliot

We're not naive about the constraints that all of us face in shaping our goals, work, and work life. There are limits. We too work in organizations and have our own stories about what we can and cannot shape. And yet, like you, we all know employees that are highly engaged and don't wait for the organization to engage them. What's the difference? They are engaged, at least in part, because they shape what they do and how they do it. They shape what is possible and acknowledge what is not possible. They recognize that the process is dynamic and continuous.

As a culminating exercise for the chapter, we invite you to take a look at your own shaping profile. The following five questions will give you a good idea of where you stand today in terms of your ability to shape your goals, your work, and your work life. Once you complete the profile, we have a list of tips for you to consider—tips that will help you improve your personal engagement through shaping. Review the tips carefully and pick out one or two that you can apply immediately.

Determine Your Shaping Profile

Respond to the statements in Table 3.6, rating your current level of engagement based on the following scale:

1 = To a very small extent
2 = To a small extent
3 = To a moderate extent
4 = To a great extent
5 = To a very great extent

TABLE 3.6   Determine Your Shaping Profile

Shaping	1. To a Very Small Extent	2. To a Small Extent	3. To a Moderate Extent	4. To a Great Extent	5. To a Very Great Extent
I have the ability to shape my work goals.	O	O	O	O	O
I have the ability to shape the work I do.	O	O	O	O	O
I have the ability to shape where and when I work.	O	O	O	O	O
I have the ability to shape whom I work with.	O	O	O	O	O
I have the ability to shape how I work.	O	O	O	O	O

Tips to Improve Engagement Through Shaping

- Plan activities in your day based on energy level (for example, creative planning in the morning and administrative work in the afternoon).
- Schedule blocks of time during the day to accomplish your work rather than allowing others to dictate your workday with meetings and phone calls.
- Practice managing your own attitude and thoughts rather than letting others and your surroundings dictate your mood.
- Work on improving things that are under your influence, and leave the rest alone.
- Write a clear vision and goals for where you want to take your career.
- Plan your activities at the beginning of every week (based on your vision and goals), then work your schedule to accomplish them.
- Look for opportunities within the company (for example, special assignments or teams) that align with your goals.
- Shape the kind of work you do based on what motivates and excites you.
- Create a flexible work schedule with your supervisor.
- Have discussions with your supervisor about how you can shape your work and work life to meet your needs and the organization's needs
- Observe and learn from what others do to customize and personalize their work.
- Consciously take time to set professional goals each year.
- Ask others what they have done to shape their organizational experience.
- Identify the things about your work life that you don't like, and work to change them to fit your needs and preferences.

Tips for Leaders

Although this book is written primarily for individual employees, we have a few tips for leaders who wish to help their employees be more engaged. The better leaders understand the six drivers, the better off the entire organization will be.

- ☐ Make sure you have a clear set of organizational goals that all employees understand. This will help employees who are setting their professional goals better align with the direction you're taking. It will create "line-of-sight" for each employee by showing how what he or she does on a daily basis links to the organization's goals.
- ☐ Before conducting a shaping discussion with an employee, reflect on the generational context of the employee. Understanding generational differences will help you understand your employees better.
- ☐ Scan your employee base for employees that might be stuck in the quicksand of dependency and deception. Invite them to discuss these potential hazards. Ask them to come back for a shaping discussion with recommendations about what they can do to shape their work productively.
- ☐ Understand each employee's concept of a career. Have each employee complete the four-step exercise in the section headed "What's Your Concept of Career?" This will give you a better sense of how your employees view their jobs.
- ☐ Once your employees have set professional goals that are aligned with the organization's goals, look for constraints and roadblocks that could get in the way of their ability to achieve the goals and work together to remove these.
- ☐ Create simple and low-cost rewards and recognition to help motivate employees to reach their goals.

☐ If you value innovation, consider giving your employees some time each week to work on new ideas to help the organization's growth and profitability.

☐ Create a "flow-friendly" environment by matching employees' passion to the job they perform.

☐ Be consistent in your shaping process. As a supervisor, you may worry about being fair to employees when you know that not all of your employees will have the chance to shape in exactly the same way. The key is to make sure the process is the same and each employee's request is fairly considered, even though the outcomes may vary.[30]

☐ Remember, it's all right to say no. Despite an employee's shaping preference, there may be job demands, customer needs, or organizational considerations that don't make flexible or preferred work assignments and arrangements possible. For example, an employee may not be ready to shape his or her organizational experience due to attendance or performance concerns. Or the timing might not be right.[31] In each case, do what you can to work with the employee to resolve these issues. Say no where you have to say no. Say yes where you can say yes.

4

Learn: Move at the Speed of Change!

"Anyone who stops learning is old, whether this happens at twenty or eighty. Anyone who keeps on learning not only remains young, but becomes constantly more valuable regardless of physical capacity."

Harvey Ullman, author

The exhilaration of learning something new is rocket fuel for employee engagement. A study of 11,000 scientists and engineers working at companies in the United States found that the desire to learn—the urge to master something new—was the best predictor of productivity. Scientists motivated by this intrinsic desire filed significantly more patents than those whose main motivation was money.[1] Do you think those scientists were engaged?

If you haven't experienced that kind of exhilaration in a while, think about the passion you had for learning when you were a child. If you can't remember, take a minute and watch young children encounter something new, like a mud puddle or a butterfly. Pay specific attention to the way they react. What's their attitude? Did you see passion? Did you see an eagerness and excitement in their eyes? Of course you did. This kind of direct learning encounter with something new is what infuses children with excitement during their formative years. It's a source of energy that makes life exciting. Learning theorist John Tagg reminds us, "Toddlers are so called because they do not fear falling down and often seem to positively enjoy it. Toddlers are all incremental theorists and embrace learning goals with gusto. And this principle that trying the currently unachievable is an intrinsically interesting endeavor drives successful enterprise at every stage of life."[2]

Do you still feel that same eagerness, or did you lose it somewhere along the way? If you're like most people, there's a good chance your passion for learning has gone south, perhaps even far south. If that's the case, read on. You'll learn how to reignite the passion for learning you once had and increase your engagement at the same time.

Where's Your Passion for Learning?

Did you know that most people lose their passion for learning as they move through the stages of life? Your journey may mirror the common pattern of decline that you see in Table 4.1.

TABLE 4.1 Typical Decline in Passion for Learning

		Preschool	Primary Grades	Middle School	High School	College/ Postsecondary	Today
7	My passion for learning is equal to or greater than what I had as a young child.	X	7	7	7	7	7
6		6	X	6	6	6	6
5		5	5	5	5	X	5
4		4	4	4	X	4	4
3		3	3	X	3	3	X
2		2	2	2	2	2	2
1	I have little to no passion for learning compared to what I had as a young child.	1	1	1	1	1	1

During your preschool years, you almost certainly had great learning passion, as most children do. During grade school, that passion probably dipped a bit, and then further declined during middle school. For most people, the passion to learn ticks back up during high school, and then goes up again during college or post-secondary training. Unfortunately, that passion drops again after college; most people don't continue a personal pattern of learning once they step out of a formal learning environment. They stop learning, with the exception of attending periodic learning events such as a workshop, seminar, or class of some kind. Here's the sad part: their passion for learning stays in the basement for the rest of their professional lives.

> *"I have no special gift. I am only passionately curious."*
> Albert Einstein

Here's the reality: learning doesn't require you to participate in an official event, but it does require you to participate. Learning is a personal process that may or may not include formal support or outside resources. At the same time, receiving formal instruction may not yield learning. The classroom has never been the sole means of real learning. Add up Abraham Lincoln's time in a formal schoolroom, and you can't total a year. But due to his insatiable appetite for learning, he maintained high passion for learning and high engagement throughout his life.

Learning is the overwhelmingly informal, and infrequently formal, process for acquiring knowledge, skills, and experience.

Peter Senge observed, "Real learning gets to the heart of what it means to be human. There is within each of us a deep hunger for this type of learning." If Senge is right, and our experience tells us he is, then real learning should be a permanent part of life—for the rest of your life.

"Live as if you were to die tomorrow. Learn as if you were to live forever."

Mahatma Gandhi

So what is real learning? It's having a new experience and then applying what we learn from that experience. If you think about it, learning has little to do with attending events or completing a course. Although learning can include formal instruction, most if it is informal. You do it on your own in the course of normal work life. It happens quietly and imperceptibly. Until you apply what you learn, it's not real. When you apply it successfully, it has a transformational effect. Any learning that culminates with improved performance feeds the innate passion we have to learn.

Here's the fundamental principle we advocate: "The single most important thing you can learn in school is how to learn when you get out of school. Why? Because once you leave school and its structured learning environment, learning for the rest of your life will overwhelmingly be based on your ability to learn on your own—without a teacher, without a classroom and without a curriculum. It will be informal learning and it will be up to you. Coming to competency will forever be your responsibility."[3]

When this principle becomes the mindset and pattern of your life, it delivers huge capacity-expanding benefits. And just in case you're interested, brain cell research confirms, "learning enhances the survival of new neurons in the adult brain. And the more engaging and challenging the problem, the greater the number of neurons that stick around."[4] This process by which the brain sprouts new neurons is called neurogenesis. Think for a minute about the implications as you consistently challenge yourself to keep learning. You will not only hang on to your existing brain cells longer, but you will also develop more of them. Here's a warning, though: inactivity does just the opposite. When neurons are not challenged with new things to learn, they slowly disappear.

"Cato, at 80, thought it proper to learn Greek."[5]

The clear pattern of highly engaged employees is that they learn constantly. They never graduate, and they don't want to. They want to keep the enthusiasm and passion. They want to retain the childlike qualities of curiosity and passion. You are never too old for butterflies and mud puddles.

Now it's your turn. Yankee baseball player and coach Yogi Berra once said, "We're lost but we're making good time." This is the state of anyone attempting to chart a personal learning path without a starting point or a path forward. Let's start with the "Passion for Learning" exercise. It will help you figure out where you are today and how to chart a path forward.

Step 1. Reflect on the six stages of your life listed across the top of Table 4.2.

Step 2. Place an X in the appropriate box to rate your passion for learning during each of the six stages of your life on a 7 to 1 scale, where 7 means "very high" and 1 means "very low."

Step 3. Draw lines between the Xs to create a trend line.

Consider where you are right now. That's your starting point. In the days ahead, refer back to this exercise to check your progress as you implement the principles you learn in this chapter. The goal, of course, is to achieve and maintain a 7 rating. That's the kind of lifelong learner you can strive to be.

TABLE 4.2   Passion for Learning Exercise

		Preschool	Primary Grades	Middle School	High School	College/ Postsecondary	Today
7	My passion for learning is equal to or greater than what I had as a young child.	7	7	7	7	7	7
6		6	6	6	6	6	6
5		5	5	5	5	5	5
4		4	4	4	4	4	4
3		3	3	3	3	3	3
2		2	2	2	2	2	2
1	I have little to no passion for learning compared to what I had as a young child.	1	1	1	1	1	1

The future is rich in possibilities for those with the passion to learn. It will be a key to your personal competitive advantage. Let's be a little more specific and ask this question: how fast do you need to be able to learn? Answer: at or above the speed of change.

Learning imperative for the highly engaged: learn at or above the speed of change.

This kind of learning agility is what allows you to innovate, execute, and adapt in any environment. If you learn at a rate that is less than the speed of change, you're in a state of professional risk and your engagement level is sure to drop. Now translate the principle to the organization. Unless an organization can learn, unlearn, and relearn at or above the speed of change, it faces the grave risk of irrelevance and failure. It simply can't survive and prosper in an environment of unrelenting change.

> *"If people don't keep learning, improving, knowing what the next issues are and continuing to be educated, they are going to fall behind."*
> Rosabeth Moss Kanter, Harvard Business School
> professor

Though all six drivers of high engagement are vital, the learning driver in particular needs to be at full throttle. It is the key to your opportunities for growth and your ability to create value in the organization. For example, Michael Lapré and Luk Van Wassenhove looked at 62 process improvement projects throughout the 1980s and 1990s in one manufacturing plant of the Belgian company Bekaert, which is the world's largest maker of steel wire. Of all the projects, "only about 25 percent delivered factory-wide improvements. Half had no bottom-line impact whatsoever and, even more surprising, the remaining 25 percent had a negative impact on the plant's overall productivity improvement."

The common characteristic of the successful projects? A focus on learning. When members of a project team saw their charter as an admonition to create new, reliable knowledge and transfer that knowledge broadly throughout the organization, the project boosted productivity. Projects with a focus on efficiency alone, however, or where learning was narrowly confined to one team or area, had no impact or a negative impact on productivity.[6]

> *"In a time of drastic change it is the learners who inherit the future. The learned usually find themselves equipped to live in a world that no longer exists."*
> Eric Hoffer, American social writer

How the World Learns

Have you ever considered how the world learns? Of course, we don't all learn in exactly the same way, but we share many of the same patterns. Unfortunately, some of those patterns are both risky and obsolete. Futurist Alvin Toffler said, "The illiterate of the twenty-first century will not be those who cannot read and write, but those who cannot learn, unlearn and relearn." Think about that for a minute. Toffler is saying that to learn, you often have to go backward before you go forward. Unlearning is your ability to identify and get rid of obsolete knowledge and skills. Relearning is your ability to rapidly pursue new knowledge and skills, the things that are current and relevant. Your success as a professional largely depends on your disposition to be agile and eager to learn.[7]

Permanent Learning

For centuries, the dominant learning model in the world was what we call permanent learning. Permanent learning means you learn things once and qualify yourself once. For example, Tim's grandfather was a locomotive engineer for the Union Pacific Railroad in the United States. He qualified himself to drive the locomotive. That skill lasted the entire span of his professional lifetime. He learned once and qualified himself permanently. His skills never became obsolete, so he continued to rely on them until he retired.

In most areas of professional life, you can't do that anymore. According to Mark L. Blazey, "The average half-life of useful knowledge is about 11 months. That means that one-half of the average employee's skills will become obsolete within 11 months. Just 20 years ago, the half-life was 18 months—approximately 50 percent greater."[8]

The pace of skill obsolescence is compounded by the accelerating scope of knowledge required to do the work that organizations do. For example, there are 100,030 clinical trials for drugs of various kinds in progress today. Can you imagine the number of new learning and unlearning requirements being generated by these clinical trials for medical professionals?

> *"Information and knowledge are the thermonuclear competitive weapons of our time."*
> Thomas Stewart, business writer, editor

According to research conducted by International Data Corporation (IDC), the world created 161 exabytes of data in 2006. That's 3 million times the amount of information contained in all the books ever written. In 2009, the size of the world's total repository of digital content was estimated at 500 billion gigabytes, or 500 exabytes. In 2010, it is estimated that we generated nearly 1,000 times that amount, or 20 percent of all digital content ever created.[9] Clearly, the pace of change varies across industry and market, but the point remains that most of us run the risk that our skills will become obsolete if we stand idly by. It's nothing less than career and engagement suicide.

> *"This higher level of anarchy will be exciting, but it will also sometimes be very painful. Entire industries will die almost overnight, laying off thousands, while others will just as suddenly appear, hungry for employees. Continuity and predictability will be the rarest of commodities."*[10]
> Michael S. Malone, business writer, editor

Continuous Learning
Fortunately, society adapted to the new conditions. About 30 years ago, the dominant learning model in advanced societies shifted from permanent learning to continuous learning. Continuous learning means that a person continues to learn for ongoing qualification. It's the idea that you have to qualify yourself on a periodic basis. You've probably heard your organization preach the mantra of continuous learning. It has now been around for more than a generation.

Dynamic Learning

But, just in the last decade, the continuous model of learning has started to give way to an even newer model. It's not good enough just to be a continuous learner anymore. Markets have become so hypercompetitive and so turbulent that you now have to be a dynamic learner (see Figure 4.1). Dynamic learning is continuous learning taken up a notch. It means your learning pattern is rapid, adaptive, collaborative, and self-directed. And guess what? When you are learning dynamically, the natural by-product is greater personal engagement in your work life and beyond.

Dynamic learners learn rapidly.[11] They don't waste time. They understand that learning is perishable; it has a shelf life. They look for change while it's still an opportunity and before it becomes a threat. When they see it coming, they immediately create a personal learning path that will help them close the new skill gaps that have opened up.

Dynamic learners are adaptive. This is where the skill of unlearning comes into play. Unlearning requires great personal effort and self-discipline. Certain things that we do over and over again

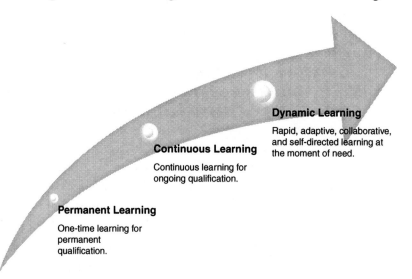

Dynamic Learning

Rapid, adaptive, collaborative, and self-directed learning at the moment of need.

Continuous Learning

Continuous learning for ongoing qualification.

Permanent Learning

One-time learning for permanent qualification.

FIGURE 4.1   The Acceleration of Learning

become so internalized that we ultimately perform them without even thinking about it. Have you ever driven home and, on arriving, realized that you can't remember making the last three turns? You were on automatic pilot. You didn't need to think about driving the car or following directions. When skills are that deeply rooted, it takes work to unlearn them. You have to perform the new way of doing something so many times that your new skills override the old way of doing things. That can often take more effort than learning something new.

Dynamic learners collaborate. They learn from and with others. They're not afraid to reveal what they don't know. They're secure in their capacity to learn, and they know that when they put their heads together with others, the chance of coming up with better solutions in less time goes up. We know from research that a person's learning capacity increases if he or she is collaborating with others. Your capacity to learn accelerates the moment you connect with the thinking of other people and tap the collective genius of the group. Collaboration allows you to drink from a reservoir of perspective and experience outside your own. In a group, you can challenge and push thinking.

Dynamic learners are self-directed. They don't surrender management or control of their learning to anyone or anything. They may choose to follow a learning path prescribed by someone else, but they never relinquish the primary responsibility to learn. They throw themselves into the learning process and do all they can to learn rapidly, adapt the learning to personal and organizational needs, and contribute and engage in the benefits of collaboration.

> "Nobody can give you an education. Education must be taken by those who want one. The will and dogged persistence of the seeker are the only essential tools needed to become educated."
>
> John Taylor Gatto, retired American schoolteacher

The six drivers of engagement overlap in dynamic learning. When they collaborate they *connect* to others. Dynamic learners *shape* their own learning. They often *stretch* themselves and move beyond their comfort zones. They consistently *achieve* meaningful outcomes. Finally, they often direct their learning in a way that *contributes* beyond themselves.

Are You a Dynamic Learner?

Now it's your turn to see how much of a dynamic learner you are. The learning self-assessment in Table 4.3 includes 10 probing questions. As you do the assessment, be completely honest with yourself so you can get an accurate picture of your learning habits and disposition. Have a "truthful encounter with reality," as we like to say. Don't be lenient. If anything, be tough. Remember, it's only when you know where you are that you can begin to work on where you want to be. And where you want to be is a rapid, adaptive, collaborative, and self-directed learner.

Step 1. Using the 7-point scale in which 1 means "not at all" and 7 means "completely," answer the 10 questions in Table 4.3 by checking the box that best describes how you approach learning.

Step 2. Add up your score and divide it by 10. The closer your average is to 7, the more dynamic you are as a learner.

Step 3. Reflect on how close or far away you are from becoming a dynamic learner. If your score is lower than you would like it to be, the rest of the chapter will help you strengthen your learning disposition and habits. As you set learning goals, this is also a great area to begin to stretch yourself and increase your personal capacity to learn.

TABLE 4.3 Learning Self-Assessment

	Not at all		A good amount		A great amount		Completely
1. To what degree do I identify my own learning needs before the organization does it for me?	1	2	3	4	5	6	7
2. To what degree do I have a personal learning plan that is independent from the organization?	1	2	3	4	5	6	7
3. To what degree do I enthusiastically see and embrace feedback?	1	2	3	4	5	6	7
4. How collaborative am I in my approach to learning?	1	2	3	4	5	6	7
5. How self-directed am I in my learning habits?	1	2	3	4	5	6	7
6. How often am I relearning?	1	2	3	4	5	6	7
7. How comfortable am I with failure?	1	2	3	4	5	6	7
8. To what degree do I use failure as an opportunity to learn?	1	2	3	4	5	6	7
9. How confident am I in saying, "I don't know"?	1	2	3	4	5	6	7
10. To what degree do I believe that it is a career risk to stop learning?	1	2	3	4	5	6	7

"I think I'm a learner. I never pretend to know all the answers, and I want to continue to be fast on my feet."
Jeffrey Immelt, CEO, General Electric

The Five Moments of Learning Need

Did you know there are five separate moments of learning need? Let's review them (see Figure 4.2), and then we'll show you how to create your own personal learning path.

1	Learning something for the *first time*.
2	Learning *more* based on prior learning experience.
3	Learning at the point of *application*.
4	Learning through adaption when things *change*.
5	Learning when things go wrong in order to *solve* a problem.

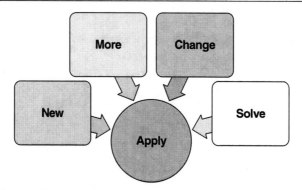

FIGURE 4.2   Learning at the Five Moments of Need
Source: Conrad A. Gottfredson and Bob Mosher, *Innovative Performance Support* (New York, McGraw-Hill, 2011).

The first moment of learning need is when you learn something for the first time—like riding a bike. The second moment of need is when you need to learn *more*. For instance, you've learned to ride the bike. Now you want to learn how to ride faster. With most skills, the organization often helps you with moments one and two—learning for the first time and learning more. After that, the organization usually steps away and you're on your own.

Here's our advice: don't expect and don't assume that the organization will help you—even with moments one and two. Why? Because, most of the time the organization won't be there to help. There are too many priorities. Things are moving too quickly. There are never enough resources. Instead, make it your personal expectation that you're in charge of your learning from the first moment of need. If the organization steps in to help, that's great.

But don't count on it. Take it upon yourself to be aggressive. Take it upon yourself to become a dynamic learner who doesn't wait for the machinery of the institution to carry you along. Don't run the risk of going on education welfare, which is an intolerably high risk. Without question, most of your learning will be informal, self-paced, and self-directed.

The third moment of need is crucial. It's the moment of *apply.* This is the moment you live in as you work. The learning challenge here is your ability to act on what you've learned. It includes planning what you will do, remembering what you may have forgotten, or adapting your performance to a unique situation. For example, you're riding that bike we talked about and suddenly a jogger dashes in front of you. The moment of apply is thrust upon you. What do you do? Hit the brakes! That is, assuming you've learned to use the brakes. The moment of apply is like that. It comes in the normal course of daily life. You may be able to choose the moment of apply and plan for it. But it is just as likely that the moment of apply will appear suddenly and you will have to respond. Both are a part of life.

The fourth moment of learning need is a unique challenge. It's the moment of *change*, and it often happens at the moment of apply that you realize that you haven't learned quite enough. Yes, you've learned how to do something, but now you're facing a different situation. No matter how well you master new knowledge or skills, you can almost bet that you will encounter a situation for which you are not fully prepared. And the only way to advance your learning is to face various situations that test and develop your learning even more. So let's get back to the bicycle. You're riding down the road and conditions change. It starts to rain. You begin braking at the next intersection, and you feel the tires sliding and losing traction beneath you. You may have read or been told about riding a bike in the rain, but you've never actually done it. So here you are at the fourth moment of need. Things have changed, and you have to learn *right now.* You let up on the brakes and regain your traction. You do it again. With practice, you learn that you need to start braking sooner and more gently. The only way to learn this is to confront the changed conditions directly.

Finally, the fifth moment of learning need is when things don't work the way they should have, could have, or were intended to. It's the moment of *solve*. Of course, this rarely happens, right? Hopefully, you're smiling when you read this. You're in good company. The fifth moment of learning need happens all the time. Sometimes it feels as if all we do is go from fifth moment to fifth moment, problem after problem. But isn't this what we do for a living—find problems and solve them? Certainly we don't plan the fifth moment of need. We don't want the fifth moment of need. It's just life. Whoops. You just got a flat tire on your bike, and you don't know how to fix it. Welcome to the fifth moment of need!

Creating a Personal Learning Path

Follow the steps outlined in this section to create a personal learning path.

Identify the Learning Gap

First, identify a learning gap in your professional life. Describe your overall learning goal and what it's going to take to close the gap. Here's an example:

> **Performance need:** I have been given the responsibility to lead a project. I've never managed a project before.
>
> **Learning gap:** I need to learn project management skills so I can successfully lead this new project.

Build a Learning Path

Next, build a learning path by reviewing each of the five moments of need. Use a "Learning Path Planning Table" to help. Table 4.4 is an example of what a completed Learning Path Planning Table might look like.

TABLE 4.4 Learning Path Planning Table

Moment of Need	Description	How Am I Going to Close the Gap?
1. **New**	When learning something for the first time	Read a book on the fundamentals of project management.
2. **More**	When learning more, expanding knowledge and skills in an area.	Take a live or online course that will walk me through the stages of setting up my project and learning how to use the basic tools of project management.
3. **Apply**	When applying what you have learned.	Ask for some coaching from a colleague who has expert project management skills. Ask her to help me get the team started by creating a formal charter for the project.
4. **Change**	When you need to unlearn an old way and learn a new way.	Stop using an outdated way of planning and scheduling. Learn how to create and use a Gantt chart with a new software program.
5. **Solve**	When things don't work as expected.	Create contingency plans for all high areas of risk. Create an alternative budget and timeline when I find that we are behind schedule and a little over budget.

"Boldness has genius, power, and magic in it."

Johann Wolfgang von Goethe

Use Your Plan to Close the Gap

Close your learning gap by acting on your plan. Action is the beginning of all progress. Your action will require the kind of boldness that Goethe described. That boldness will help you find the best sources of knowledge and skill to close the learning gap. Never relinquish primary control over your learning path. Seek counsel from those you trust. Take full advantage of what your organization has to offer, but don't rely on anyone or anything else to define your learning path. Sometimes, an organization will impose learning expectations or even mandates. But if at any point in your learning journey you determine that a prescribed learning path isn't helpful, or that there is a more effective way, have a shaping discussion with your manager about it. Propose a better and more effective learning path for yourself.

Adapt and Adjust

Adapt and adjust as you move down the path. If part of your learning path isn't delivering results, drop it. If something else makes better sense, do it. Never let the fear of failure hinder your learning progress. If you fail, make the effort to learn from it. That's what John Chambers, the CEO of Cisco, did as a young child. Challenged by dyslexia, he struggled to read. While all the other kids in his class read from left to right, Chambers met his challenge by learning to read from right to left. That formative experience taught him to become a dynamic learner. Today, when Chambers hires a new employee, he asks first about results and then about failures. "People think of us as a product of our successes," he observes. "I'd actually argue that we're a product of the challenges we faced in life. And how we handled those challenges probably had more to do with what we accomplish in life."[12] When failure knocks on your door, recognize it for what it can be—a fruitful learning experience.

Your success is based on your effort and judgment throughout the process. This is where the power of others can really help. Don't attempt to go it alone. As you move forward to create a learning path and then implement it, seek input and candid feedback. This is a fundamental principle that will not only breathe life into the process, but accelerate it and protect you against dumb mistakes. Feedback is the life force of real learning. It is, as the chalkboard aphorism suggests, the breakfast of champions. Do you really believe that?

Is Feedback Really the Breakfast of Champions?

Michael Gelb, an expert in creativity and innovation, made this statement: "Champions know that success is inevitable, that there is no such thing as failure, only feedback." What, exactly, does this statement mean? Any time we fail to perform optimally, we experience a degree of failure. We may get the job done but fail to get all the results we wanted. And sometimes, we fail miserably. In all cases, it's important to seek the kind and level of feedback that will help us improve future performance. When you experience performance failure to any degree, you face two options: learn or don't. Dynamic learners never squander the opportunity to learn, even if it means swallowing their ego. With solid feedback and a willingness to act on it, success is inevitable.

> *"One of the reasons people stop learning is that they become less and less willing to risk failure."*
>
> John Gardner

Isn't it interesting how different we are as humans when it comes to receiving feedback? Some of us don't want any. We become defensive. We bristle and buck. We get angry or resentful. We refuse to consider the possibility that another person might be able to shed light on our performance and help us improve. Yet the highest performers in almost every field of endeavor are used to a diet rich in feedback. Most are grateful and gracious when they receive it, especially when it is candid and helpful. They treat it as a precious gift.

Take Cael Sanderson. Cael was a wrestler at Iowa State University. In four years of competition, he compiled a record of 159 wins and 0 losses, an athletic feat never before accomplished in his sport. He then went on to win the gold medal in freestyle wrestling for the United States at the 2004 Olympic Games in Athens. But what intrigues us most about Cael is his learning disposition. We interviewed Cael and were amazed at his insight into the learning process. He said wrestling provides constant feedback. He made it his goal to learn faster than his competition. "You have to be open in order to learn," he said. "A lot of people simply aren't willing to ask for feedback or act on it. You have to overcome your own pride in order to get better."[13] Cael maintains this dynamic learning approach, and it's paying off. He is now the head wrestling coach at Pennsylvania State University. In only his second year as head coach, he and his team won the NCAA national championship.

> *"I am always learning and working at the margin of my ignorance."*
> Harvey Golub, chairman, Campbell Soup Company

Obviously, there's an emotional component to receiving feedback. It requires courage and humility to seek, listen, and act. But guess what? If you have any interest in improving your skills quickly and efficiently, you avoid feedback at your peril. Highly engaged employees are more open to feedback than the average employee. Why? Because they've discovered its accelerating power. Take yourself out of your work setting for a minute. Think of any skill or talent you've tried to develop—in music, sports, the arts, or whatever. How has feedback helped you improve that talent?

Think about the athletic arena. Pick any sport—from baseball to soccer, from tennis to tae kwon do. Everywhere you look, you find coaches. We just take it as a given. We don't even question the fact that in sports, if you want to improve performance, you need a coach and you need clear and targeted feedback. And not just a little bit, but generous amounts of feedback. Without it, you'll be slow and make limited progress.

Alan Fine offers this critical insight: "Typically, the biggest obstacle in performance isn't not knowing what to do; it's not doing what we know. In other words, the problem is not as much about knowledge acquisition as it is about knowledge execution."[14] It's a motivation problem more than an ability problem. And that's what good coaches do. They observe your performance and give constant feedback as a way to help you improve your execution. They might tell you what you're doing that's right, but they spend most of their time focusing on what you need to do to improve your performance.

Ask yourself this penetrating question: How's your relationship with feedback? What's your attitude toward coaching? If you want to stay where you are, or grow slowly with flaws hanging on longer than needed, ignore the opportunity for feedback. You might get by for a while, but ultimately you will fail to learn at or above the speed of change. At some point, you will be outdistanced and outperformed by someone who has learned how to seek and receive feedback. All of our research confirms that in the professional workplace, feedback accelerates performance just as it does in the field of athletics.

Develop a Personal Feedback Loop

The principle of feedback is governed by a very simple principle: if you wait around for it, you'll get very little of it. Here's a four-step process to enrich your professional experience with more feedback (see Figure 4.3).

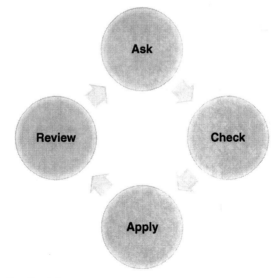

FIGURE 4.3 Feedback Loop

Step 1: Ask

You've got to want feedback, and you have to seek it. Why? Because most people won't give it unless they're asked. And even if they are asked, most people are hesitant. That's human nature. Giving and receiving feedback adds risk to a relationship. No wonder people hesitate on both sides. You have to ask, and you have to keep asking. But don't ask just anyone. If you want to accelerate your performance and become better at what you are learning to do, ask for feedback from someone you trust and from someone who knows how to give it. The best feedback is immediate, specific, and actionable. The worst kind is delayed, general, and theoretical. Make sure the feedback you get is from credible and candid sources.

Also, keep in mind that you don't need feedback about everything, nor do you need the same level of feedback whenever you seek it. You need to seek feedback systematically and at a pace that allows you the room to act upon it. A good rule of thumb is to seek feedback according to how critical the impact of failure in an area could be to you, others, or your organization. Table 4.5 provides an example of how you could do this.

When you call on the time and skills of another person to provide feedback, it should be worth that person's time and yours. Remember, never be threatened by feedback. Seek it diligently. Meaningful feedback is your best friend as you learn with the intent of improving your performance.

Step 2: Check

Ensure that the feedback you receive is accurate and helpful. The primary reason you should check the feedback and verify its value is that most people dismiss feedback too quickly. Dismissing feedback is a natural inclination. It's especially true when feedback comes unvarnished or uninvited. If you ever find yourself becoming defensive as you receive feedback, pay particular attention to it and ask yourself these questions:

1. Is this person sincerely trying to help me?

TABLE 4.5 Critical Impact Rating Scale

How critical are the consequences of failure?						
1	**2**	**3**	**4**	**5**	**6**	**7**
Minimal Impact		**Moderate Impact**		**Significant Impact**		**Catastrophic Impact**
The consequences are negligible. No impact on outcome. I can readily recover. No impact on others. There could be some decrease in workflow efficiencies and/ or increase in workload.		The consequences will not threaten successful performance. The event may impact the attitudes and workload of others. If there is reputation or monetary loss, it would create moderate or temporary harm, damage, or loss to the organization.		Consequences will require significant commitment of resources and/or lasting consequences for others. Significant harm to individuals and the organization with potentially permanent consequences. Adverse impact on work environment and culture. Significant compromise to relationships within and outside the organization.		Consequences cause major problems for others and/or the organization. Impact on reputation will be long-term, and might be irreparable in terms of damage or loss. Compromise of professional status, reputation, and ability to do the work. Long-term compromise to relationships within and outside of the organization.

2. Is this person a credible source?
3. How might this feedback help me?

If the answer to any of these questions is yes, then listen carefully. Take notes. Express appreciation. Consider its importance to your performance before you dismiss any part of it. If you are receiving feedback on a critical skill (see Table 4.5), check it by reviewing it with a second or third credible source. Always verify feedback on your performance before accepting or dismissing it.

> *"The problem in my life and other people's lives is not the absence of knowing what to do, but the absence of doing it."*
>
> Peter Drucker

Step 3: Apply

Performance growth happens as you apply feedback over time. One of the qualities you have as a human being is the ability to step back and objectively look at your own performance. As you do this, consider the feedback you receive from others. But you can also provide yourself feedback. Whenever you do this objectively, it becomes the most effective feedback you will ever receive. Self-evaluation can accelerate personal growth more effectively than any other feedback source. Here are some guiding principles to help you do this:

1. Focus first on successful performance. Did you accomplish what you set out to accomplish? If not or if only partially, what interfered? How would you counter those interferences given another opportunity?
2. Look for inefficiencies. How could you have achieved successful performance in less time, with less effort, or with fewer resources?
3. Check for missed opportunities. What else could or should you have done?
4. Assess the quality of results. How beneficial were your efforts? What potential benefits were missed?

Put the feedback you receive alongside your own assessment and establish a plan to apply whatever is relevant to your performance. Keep after it until the new way of performing is second nature.

Step 4: Review

After you apply the feedback that you have received, take time to review the results. Did things go better? Worse? How? Why? What are you going to do now? Engagement rises when you see your actions leading to results and creating impact. Once you've done this, you're ready to repeat the cycle and continue to improve your learning and performance with feedback.

These four steps provide an initial framework to help you aggressively seek and know how to process feedback. Study them, and then allow yourself time to apply the principles in a way that works for you.

> *"Education is not filling a bucket, but lighting a fire."*
> William Butler Yeats

Conclusion

Dynamic learners create personal learning paths, move fast to close their learning gaps, and establish rigorous feedback loops. As you apply the principles introduced in this chapter, you have a chance to rekindle your passion for learning and become the dynamic learner you need to be. You have the chance to prosper in the new normal and watch your engagement soar.

> *"I am still learning. That is an important mark of a good leader . . . to know you don't know it all and never will."*
> Anne Mulcahy, former chairman and CEO, Xerox

Remember that when an organization adjusts to the external pressures of change, the skills, knowledge, and job roles within the organization must change as well. Carry with you the expectation that your job role requirements could change at any time. As the HR Policy Association states, "Career paths are constantly shifting as new technologies, new industries and new work processes replace older ones at an increasingly rapid pace. In fact, because of the pace of today's economies, companies often change more quickly than many of their employees can adapt to that change."[15]

If you've become a dynamic learner, you're well prepared. If you're interested in performing at a high level, climbing the leadership ladder, or simply keeping your job, you need to get used to the idea that you must be able to lead by how you learn. The new relationship between learning and leading may be the single biggest development in the field of leadership in our time. In the new normal, an organization's competitive advantage is tied directly to its ability to learn. You have to learn at or above the speed of change and then model it for others. The very process of learning feeds your personal engagement and increases your productive contribution. You become more valuable to the organization because of your ability to influence others to become dynamic learners.

> *"I am always doing that which I cannot do, in order that I may learn how to do it."*
>
> Picasso

Highly engaged employees cultivate the disposition and behavior of a dynamic learner. They consistently apply the third driver of high engagement—learning. How about you? Whether you need to make some minor adjustments or radical changes to your personal learning patterns, do it. You'll experience the exhilaration of learning. The passion will come back—that passion for mud puddles and butterflies.

Tips for Leaders

The most important thing you can do to help others increase their engagement through learning is to model dynamic learning yourself. You have to lead by how you learn. This will create a climate that encourages those you lead to do the same.

The relationship between learning and leading is something you can't pull apart. You can't lead effectively if you're not learning yourself. And you can't lead effectively if you're not helping others learn. John F. Kennedy said, "Leadership and learning are indispensable to each other."

Leading through learning implies a level of humility and curiosity that is foreign to a traditional model of leadership in which the leader is the expert. It asks leaders to develop confidence in the very act of not knowing. It challenges leaders to learn each time reality steps ahead of them. It puts the burden of learning at or above the speed of change squarely on your shoulders as a leader. You can't fake it or delegate it. Ask yourself the questions in Table 4.6, which will determine your readiness to lead by how you learn.

TABLE 4.6   How Do You Model Learning? (Continued)

Leading by How I Learn	1. To a Very Small Extent	2. To a Small Extent	3. To a Moderate Extent	4. To a Great Extent	5. To a Very Great Extent
How prepared are you for the transition from the "leader as expert" paradigm to one that emphasizes the "leader as learner"?	O	O	O	O	O
To what extent is your personal credibility based on your personal learning agility as opposed to old knowledge and skills?	O	O	O	O	O
How much do you lean on the machinery of your organization to govern your personal learning path? To what degree are you on educational welfare?	O	O	O	O	O
How effective are you at calling forth the discretionary efforts and creative potential of other people through the influence of your learning habits, curiosity, and enthusiasm in the face of problems that don't yet have answers?	O	O	O	O	O
How effective are you at engaging and mobilizing people based on your influence skills without hiding behind the artifacts of title, position, and authority in order to press people into service?	O	O	O	O	O

(Continued)

TABLE 4.6   (Continued)

Leading by How I Learn	1. To a Very Small Extent	2. To a Small Extent	3. To a Moderate Extent	4. To a Great Extent	5. To a Very Great Extent
To what degree are you psychologically prepared to show your vulnerability to incompetence as your skills become outdated because you have the ability to learn and adapt?	O	O	O	O	O
If competence is a matter of individual learning agility, to what degree are you preparing for the new environment?	O	O	O	O	O
To what degree do you believe that learning is where advantage comes from, that it represents the highest form of enterprise risk management, and that the biggest risk a firm can take is to cease to learn?	O	O	O	O	O

You have already done the 10-question self-assessment for determining the degree to which you are a dynamic learner. Take a look at the associated bulleted suggestions under each question to guide your efforts in supporting those you lead.

1. To what degree do I identify my own learning needs before the organization does it for me?
   □ Encourage independent learning paths as you set expectations for personal development
2. To what degree do I have a personal learning plan that is independent from the organization?
   □ Resist prescribing a learning path. Open the door for learning and growth opportunities outside the formal options in your organization.
3. To what degree do I enthusiastically see and embrace feedback?
   □ Demonstrate a disposition to seek and receive candid feedback.
   □ Facilitate peer coaching and review opportunities.

4. How collaborative am I in my approach to learning?
   - □ Give employees the option to share their learning plans with each other and make provisions for collaborative learning time.
5. How self-directed am I in my learning habits?
   - □ Acknowledge and reward successes where employees have demonstrated independent learning in the process.
6. How often am I relearning?
   - □ Encourage and put in place quick reference options whenever employees are asked to change their performance pattern in a given area.
7. How comfortable am I with failure?
   - □ At the project level, set boundaries for acceptable and unacceptable failure.
8. To what degree do I use failure as an opportunity to learn?
   - □ Establish a "lessons learned" option for each project for gathering meaningful insights to improve future efforts.
9. How confident am I in saying, "I don't know"?
   - □ Facilitate collaboration as a means for your team members to safely address "not knowing."
10. To what degree do I believe that it is a career risk to stop learning?
    - □ Recognize and reward dynamic learning patterns as they emerge.

5

Stretch: Go to Your Outer Limits!

"Growth and comfort do not coexist."

Virginia Rometty, CEO, IBM

Jan-Jan Lam left her native Taipei, Taiwan, to begin graduate study at the University of South Carolina. When she boarded the plane, she said good-bye to family, friends, a familiar culture, and a predictable and happy life. When she stepped off the plane, she faced the prospect of strangers, a foreign language, limited financial resources, and culture shock. The move pushed Jan-Jan suddenly and dramatically out of her comfort zone. Why did she do it? In Jan-Jan's case, she wanted to improve her family's quality of life. Day by day, she diligently applied herself. Eventually, the days turned into years. Then one day she donned a cap and gown and was handed a diploma. It was graduation day, and she had done it.

Jan-Jan found a good job in the healthcare industry. It offered stability and a chance to move up. But as it turned out, her family decided to follow her and immigrate to the United States. Suddenly, she had to support more than herself. With zero experience in the industry, Jan-Jan quit her job and opened a restaurant.

She thought it would be the best way to provide jobs for her family members. "I can figure it out," she would say to herself. Together, she and her family members learned, sacrificed, and made it work. If that weren't enough, Jan-Jan took on the added challenge of running a struggling software company that another family member had started. In both endeavors, she succeeded.

Through her stretching experiences, Jan-Jan improved her skills and increased her capability. After leading these two successful ventures, she decided to seek a new challenge. What she really wanted was to lead people in an organization that had a compelling mission, something that would stir her passion. She found what she was looking for in one of the largest media and entertainment conglomerates in the world. But she had to start at the bottom just to get in the door. She landed a job managing a restaurant at one of the company's amusement parks. It was a big step down in income but, in her mind, a step up in opportunity.

Jan-Jan applied the same resolve and determination. She stretched herself to learn a whole new industry. Before long, she was managing one of the largest food service operations in the company. But this wasn't where she wanted to be. She knew she could do more. When a posting for a six-month project opportunity in the education and training department appeared, she jumped at it, believing the temporary assignment could open the door to more opportunity. During the project, she realized the organization needed someone with measurement expertise. She boldly walked into her manager's office and proposed that the company create a new position to fill the void. The company agreed, and when the leaders realized Jan-Jan had a degree in statistics, they appointed her to fill the new post.

Jan-Jan continued this pattern of stretching and moved to even higher levels of responsibility. Today, she leads one of the world's most innovative learning and development organizations, an organization that designs and develops training solutions for more than 80,000 employees. She recently accepted a new assignment

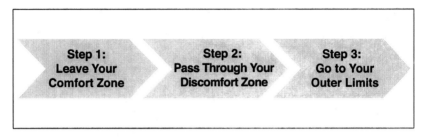

FIGURE 5.1   The Stretching Process

to plan and lead the implementation of all training required to bring onboard new employees for a multibillion-dollar operation in Shanghai, China, the city where her parents were born.

Jan-Jan's success in professional life is directly traceable to her core disposition to leave her comfort zone, pass through her discomfort zone, and push to the outer limits of her capability. This process is known as stretching (Figure 5.1), and it's a basic driver of high engagement.

Stretching is the process of getting out of your comfort zone, passing through your discomfort zone, and pushing to your outer limits.

Our study of highly engaged people like Jan-Jan reveals a consistent pattern: highly engaged people show a willingness to stretch. And there are attending benefits. Stretching increases your capacity, raises your performance level, creates opportunity, and, of course, elevates engagement.

In our research, we found a direct correlation between stretching and engagement. Stretching means putting forth effort. Those who put forth effort in their professional lives are more engaged. Likewise, those who put forth enormous effort are likely to be enormously engaged.

If you're willing to stretch, you can apply the other drivers. If you're not, you're stuck. Here's the problem: another person can't get you unstuck. You have to do it yourself. Engagement is like that. It's one of those things in life you have to do mostly for yourself.

Stretch to Increase Your Capacity

Stretching leads to increased capacity. In fact, you can't build capacity inside your comfort zone any more than a baby bird can learn to fly inside the nest. You have to give yourself permission to leave the nest. Think about what that means. If you're willing to stretch, your capacity is unlimited.

Take sports, for instance. You can't stay in your comfort zone and achieve a pattern of winning. You have to go to your outer limits. According to Phil Gallagher, director of the Applied Physiology Laboratory at the University of Kansas, elite competitive cyclists develop stronger hearts that can push more blood per heartbeat and oxygenate the blood more efficiently than recreational cyclists' hearts do. In addition, Gallagher has measured the energy output of cyclists using a power meter that gives cyclist productivity in watts. His research shows that elite cyclists can double their physical capacity to generate physical energy through extreme training. Elite cyclists can generate 450 watts of average power as they bike compared to about 200 watts for normal cyclists.[1]

Yet the benefits of stretching aren't limited to athletics. Depending on the nature of your stretching activity, you can expand your mental, emotional, social, and physical capacities. Your capacity won't increase on its own. You have to stretch on purpose. We're talking about stretching by design.

In all aspects of professional life, stretching is the only way to increase capacity. It's a chance to raise your agility, increase your intelligence, strengthen your interpersonal skills, enlarge your physical endurance, broaden your understanding, and hone your judgment.

"The only way of finding the limits of the possible is by going beyond them into the impossible."
                                        Arthur C. Clark, science fiction writer

What's fascinating is that there's no alternative to stretching. You can't perform above your capacity simply because you want to. You have to stretch first.

Stretch to Increase Your Performance

We're not going to lie. Stretching creates discomfort, especially in the short term. But it gets better. It becomes exhilarating in the long term. It's an interesting sort of bittersweet, agony-and-ecstasy combination. We suspect you've experienced both the discomfort and the exhilaration of stretching in your own life.

Did you know that Thomas Edison held 1,093 U.S. patents? Edison was a person who lived his entire professional life in a stretching mode. Do you think he was highly engaged? It's a silly question, isn't it? The man seemed to be totally engaged all of the time. Aside from being a prolific inventor, he's a fantastic case study of a person who built capacity in himself and others through his willingness to stretch.

At one point in his life, he was struggling to invent the light-bulb and had failed to do it after more than 9,000 experiments. A young reporter caught up with him and asked him if he felt like a failure. Edison replied, "Young man, why would I feel like a failure? And why would I ever give up? I now know definitively over 9,000 ways that an electric light bulb will not work. Success is almost in my grasp." Just a little while later, and after more than 10,000 attempts, Edison invented the lightbulb.

If you're stretching, you're going to fail along the way. As Denzel Washington said in his commencement speech at the

University of Pennsylvania, "If you don't fail, you are not even trying." But that's okay. Even if you do fail, the process of stretching rewards you with increased capacity.

But there's another benefit of stretching: When you stretch, it helps other people stretch. Effort and motivation are contagious, so your stretching creates lift for those around you. In his time, Edison set up the world's first large-scale research and development center in West Orange, New Jersey. At the time, it was the largest scientific testing laboratory in the world. How many other people were led to stretch because Edison first stretched?

Today Laura Cinat leads major transformational change at Kraft Foods, and she relishes the challenge. Every initiative presents a stretch assignment. Yet she admits that often her professional stretching doesn't compare to the stretching she does as a mother of two daughters who constantly push her to her outer limits.

She recently taught herself to sew so that she could make the costumes for her seven-year-old daughter's school play. In addition to all the stretching she does as a mother, Laura also cares for ailing parents and a sister who is disabled from an automobile accident. If that isn't enough, she manages the estate of another sister, who prior to her untimely death was director of the UC Irvine Regional Burn Center. When you meet Laura, you immediately sense a woman of enormous capacity. It makes you wonder where her capacity came from. So we had to ask. That's where it gets even more interesting.

After completing her MBA at the University of Michigan, Laura voluntarily left her comfort zone and applied for a position with the university's MBA Enterprise Corps. She was given a 15-month assignment in Kiev, Ukraine. With no previous language experience, Laura spent her first three months in Ukraine learning the language and immersing herself in the culture. She spent eight hours a day studying at the local business center and opted to stay with a family that didn't speak English. Most of the time, as she recounts, she didn't know what was being said. It was a difficult environment, to say the least. Her living conditions were humble. She had no privacy. Hot water was a luxury, and she had no idea what was in the food. This constant lack of predictability proved to be an instructive part of her stretch experience. In her words, "These things proved to be the most invigorating part of the whole experience."

After she had learned the language and the culture, the excitement began to fade for Laura. She had stretched herself to her outer limits and now began to feel stale and underutilized. So she decided to take another stretch assignment. She volunteered to travel throughout the country speaking and motivating women to start and grow their own businesses. The Iron Curtain had only recently fallen. People were excited and yet filled with anxiety. At the time, she was a 29-year-old woman from Canada trying to influence people who didn't always trust her. But she persevered and eventually earned the trust of women throughout the country. On her thirtieth birthday, her Ukrainian colleagues presented her with a special jewelry box as a symbol of the trust and friendship she had gained with people a continent away. After Kiev, Laura spent another year and a half in Ukraine working on other challenging projects. Her experiences taught her defining lessons that she uses today in her efforts to lead major initiatives at Kraft Foods.

Out of high school, I (Tim Clark) took a scholarship to play Division I college football. As a new freshman football player, I was lifting weights one day and I asked our strength coach how many repetitions I should do on the bench press. With a puzzled look, he replied, "What do you mean, how many reps? Go until you hit muscle failure." He was saying lift the weight as many times as you can until your muscles literally collapse. Now that's not always the right advice, but in this case it was. He wanted me to make a step-change improvement in my strength, and so I needed to stretch as far as I could. I needed to go to my outer limits—the place where new capacity is built.

Stretch to Increase Your Opportunities

Stretching creates opportunity. It helps you create your own luck. It's a disposition that delivers value. It helps prepare you for the unknown and steels you against discouragement. It cultivates a tenacity you can't get in any other way.

In 1992, 15-year-old Newton Peter Gborway fled his home in Liberia into the night jungle, hoping to reach the Sierra Leone border. In one of Africa's bloodiest civil wars, rebel soldiers were conscripting boys his age and killing those who refused to enlist and join their cause. On one occasion, while in a refugee camp, Peter stepped away from a group of boys to search for something to eat. During his brief absence, rebels entered the camp and executed his friends. At one point, he hitched a ride, but there was no room to sit in the car, so he mounted himself on the top of a luggage rack. For 97 miles Peter struggled to hang on as the car bounded over dusty roads and swerved around corners at high speeds. His daring flight pushed him to his outer limits.

Peter's efforts to contact his family ended with reports that his family had been killed and their home burned. Peter carried on and over the next 10 years made his way from Sierra Leone to Guinea, and then to Dakar, Senegal, on to Cape Verde, and finally to Botswana, where he faced being jailed or sent back to Liberia. His only escape was to enroll in school, which he did with the help of friends.

Peter was without home, family, or country, but he refused to give up. Every step of the way, he worked to stay alive and make something of himself. With the fear, loneliness, and doubt that plagued his life, there simply was no comfort zone. It was a constant state of stretch. He persevered against staggering odds and miraculously obtained a visa to pursue his education in the United States. He continued to overcome challenges and eventually completed a master's degree in social work. For 19 years Peter never lost hope of finding his family. He recently returned to Liberia and was miraculously reunited with his mother, three sisters, and two brothers, all of whom had been falsely reported to be dead.

Peter is the first to admit that he could never have accomplished what he did without the help of others. Along the way, people opened doors of opportunity for Peter. Why? Not only did they want to help, but they saw in him a willingness to stretch, which made them more willing to help. People and organizations tend to behave that way. They value those who demonstrate a disposition and pattern of stretching. If people believe their efforts to help will be appreciated and acted on, they're more likely to lend a hand.

As the realities of the twenty-first century challenge organizations, those organizations will increasingly reward those who demonstrate a willingness to stretch. Those who steadfastly resist stretching, those who hole themselves up in their comfort zones, will find themselves passed over. Just ask yourself, whom would you invest in? Someone who stretches or someone who slacks?

> *"It takes courage to push yourself to places that you have never been before...to test your limits...to break through barriers. And the day came when the risk it took to remain tight inside the bud was more painful than the risk it took to blossom."*
>
> Anaïs Nin

Stretch to Increase Engagement

There's a point during the stretching process when you start to get it. You begin the transition from discomfort to exhilaration. Sometimes the exhilaration you feel is so intense that you enter a condition called *flow*. Psychologist Mihaly Csikszentmihalyi coined this term from his research on high-performing people. You know you're in a flow state when you feel consumed in an activity. "You often have an incredible sense of concentration, involvement, high performance, and control. Some report experiencing a state of focused energy or a transcendent state of wellbeing, and an altered sense of time."[2]

Csikszentmihalyi interviewed an elite cyclist who described what it was like to be in a flow state during the grueling last seven-kilometer climb of the 1,500-mile Tour de France. He said, "I was totally absorbed, 110 percent; that was all that mattered in the whole existence. It just amazed me how I could maintain such high concentration for three hours. I'm used to having my mind wander, especially under pressure. Afterward, I couldn't come down, I was on a high. I felt like I wanted to go ride up that hill again."[3]

Almost anyone can experience the exhilaration of flow. It fuels engagement and as a result makes life more satisfying. It motivates you to stretch again. At some point, you find yourself in a state of perpetual growth because stretching has become enjoyable, even natural, and a part of everyday life. Each new stretch builds on the last, and you begin to feel what it's like to have a sustained level of high engagement.

Stretch to Survive and Thrive

If you're still not convinced that stretching is for you, consider the risk of not stretching in the twenty-first century. In a time when change is ever-present, those who fail to stretch, those who turn away from challenging growth opportunities, are putting their personal competitive advantage at risk. No matter how gifted or talented you may be, if you remain idle in your comfort zone, your capacity atrophies. Intelligence alone won't be enough. As Stanford psychologist Carol Dweck has observed, "There is no relation between students' abilities or intelligence and the development of mastery-oriented qualities. Some of the very brightest students avoid challenges, dislike effort, and wilt in the face of difficulty. And some of the less bright students are real go-getters, thriving on challenge, persisting intensely when things get difficult and accomplishing more than you expected."[4]

When it comes to capacity building and its associated impact on engagement, you either grow or regress. Stretching is the difference between a vibrant or stagnant life, between an energetic or listless attitude, between soaring or diminishing engagement levels, between exemplary or lackluster job performance. In *The Sun Also Rises*, Ernest Hemingway's character Mike Campbell, when asked how he went bankrupt, replies, "Gradually and then suddenly." That is the most likely pattern for the disengaged who would rather lounge in their comfort zones.

> *"Only those who will risk going too far can possibly find out how far one can go."*
>
> T. S. Eliot

One day, business school graduate Garner Kronschnabel decided to abandon his comfort zone. He left his 10-year marketing position at his father's company, sold his home and car, and moved to Seattle, Washington. He knew most everyone in his hometown. He knew no one in Seattle. He left his lifelong friends and went to a place where he was a total stranger.

He had left a great job for no job. But Garner had two passions: flying and boating. He decided he wanted a profession that would satisfy these passions and determined that he would become a floatplane pilot, so he enrolled in a flight course and began looking for a job. He soon found a seasonal marketing position at a regional airline with a fleet of floatplanes. Garner stretched to learn the business. He traveled with the pilots when he had time off and did all he could to learn from them. When he finished his summer job, the company offered him a full-time job. We don't yet know the rest of the story, but Garner continues to stretch himself in anticipation of one day piloting his very own floatplane. His disposition to stretch has allowed him to survive at first. In the end, it will allow him to thrive.

The Four Patterns of Stretching

When it comes to stretching, highly engaged people tend to demonstrate four consistent patterns of behavior.

Pattern 1: They Leave Their Comfort Zones

The highly engaged consistently leave their comfort zones. No one progresses in a perpetual state of comfort. In your comfort zone, things tend to be familiar, controlled, and predictable. You feel confident and satisfied in the knowledge and abilities you have. Although you may be working hard, nothing you do feels too difficult or overwhelming. The highly engaged, on the other hand, simply can't abide staying in their comfort zones. It might be comfortable, but it gets boring. As one 92-year-old lifelong stretcher told us, "If heaven is a place of peace and rest, then send me to hell." Serious stretchers don't wait for anyone or anything to push them out of their comfort zones. They do it on their own.

> *"In life, we face difficulties and hardships because life is about striving. The people who are going to succeed are those who are able to push that extra mile, despite knowing that every sinew is at its limits."*
>
> Jasper Tong, author

Pattern 2: They Are Willing to Endure Discomfort

The highly engaged are willing to endure sustained discomfort. Here's what the discomfort zone and your outer limits can offer:

- Delayed gratification
- Exhaustion
- Insecurity
- Failure

- Discouragement
- Frustration
- Stress

Why would anyone choose to leave his or her comfort zone only to be lavished with these kinds of rewards? Answer: they understand these results are temporary and yet required for personal growth. They also understand that, generally speaking, the greater the discomfort, the greater the reward.

> *"The pain you feel today will be the strength you feel tomorrow."*
>
> Robert Moore, bodybuilder

Pattern 3: They Learn from Experience

The highly engaged learn from the entire experience. Obviously you can't pitch your tent in the outer limits campground. Yes, that's where you build new capacity, but you can also burn yourself out. You have to replenish energy and renew yourself. Highly engaged people learn to balance stretching with renewal. Figuratively speaking, disengaged people simply want to stay home and watch TV. The difference is that for people who don't want to stretch, much of life becomes a pain-avoidance strategy. In the end, you get what you want. Highly engaged people make things happen. Disengaged people often watch what engaged people do from their living rooms.

Basketball legend Michael Jordan put it this way: "I've missed more than 9,000 shots in my career. I've lost almost 300 games. Twenty-six times I've been trusted to take the game-winning shot and missed. I've failed over and over and over again in my life. And that is why I succeed." Perhaps it's possible to close your eyes and grit your teeth as you make your way through your discomfort zone. The tragedy would be to do nothing but complain about it and not learn anything.

> *"It is impossible to live without failing at something, unless you live so cautiously that you might as well not have lived at all—in which case, you fail by default."*
> J. K. Rowling, author of the Harry Potter series

Pattern 4: They Get Comfortable Stretching

The highly engaged get comfortable stretching. In sports, we don't stop training. It's how we keep our current level of performance and then move to the next. We have to stretch again and again in order to consolidate our gains. Keeping what we earn is never free. It requires ongoing time and effort. For instance, Steve Nash is the highest career percentage free throw shooter in the National Basketball Association at 90 percent. How many free throws a day do you think he takes to maintain that level of performance? When you get a chance, check out a YouTube video of his shooting workouts. It will blow you away to see how hard the guy works every day to maintain his skill level.

> *"One's mind, once stretched by a new idea, never regains its original dimensions."*
> Oliver Wendell Holmes

Failing Forward

If you stretch, you're bound to succeed. You're also bound to fail. In fact, you're going to fail more than you succeed. Your life, as Teddy Roosevelt said, is going to be "checkered with failure." But that's better than not trying at all. Stretching provides the fringe benefits of failure. Even when you don't succeed, you actually do. You take what you learn with you. It's not the failure itself that's so valuable, it's the by-product—the residual lessons and experience that you gain in the process. Inevitably, what you see in people who succeed more than most is that they try more than most, which also means that they have more failures. But they're not afraid of that.

Edmund Phelps, a Nobel Prize winner in economics, once made the statement, "In any organization of the economy, the participants will score unequally in how far they manage to go in their personal growth."[5] The reason is simply that some people are willing to leave their comfort zones and others are not.

Your comfort zone is a place of familiarity. It's what you know. It's where you have confidence, competence, and comfort. But with time, your comfort zone has less and less to offer except idle contentment. It offers you less challenge, less stimulation, and therefore, less personal growth. You may find yourself content in your comfort zone, but chances are that you're less engaged. It's in our comfort zones that we get lazy and apathetic. We don't feel good about ourselves because we know we can do better and be better. Outside our comfort zone, we grow even if we don't succeed. A dramatic example of this is what we call the "Mount Everest principle."

More than 4,000 people have attempted to climb to the top of Mount Everest, the largest peak in the world at 29,029 feet. Only 460 have made it. That's less than a 12 percent success rate. But for the other 88 percent who don't summit, is it really a failure? They come away from the experience with newfound confidence, determination, and understanding. These are the fringe benefits of failure. These are the rewards you take with you. The Mount Everest principle teaches us that when we stretch, our chance of failing is higher than our chance of succeeding. Over the long run, trying and failing become the cornerstones of personal development. The key is to summon the courage to get out there. As business professor Robert Sutton likes to say, "Failure sucks, but instructs"—that is, if we can learn from it.

To ensure that our stretching isn't wasted effort, that we fail forward, there are a few things to keep in mind:

1. **Give yourself room to fail.** If there's absolutely no margin for error, you will try to avoid trying in the first place. Set up conditions that give you some permission to learn and make mistakes along the way.

2. **Give yourself limits to fail.** You also need to know what kind of failure you and the organization can manage and tolerate. Set limits so that when you fail, it's predictable and bounded failure. This makes it safer and takes a lot of fear and uncertainty out of the process.

3. **Review your performance.** Ask yourself what went well and not so well. Take the time to reflect deeply on the experience. Talk about it with the people involved. The more candid and probing the discussion, the faster you learn and the better your performance the next time.

"Ever tried. Ever failed. No matter. Try again. Fail again. Fail better."

Samuel Beckett, poet, playwright

The Stretching Process

When you learn the process of stretching, you appreciate it more. And you appreciate people who exhibit a pattern of stretching in their lives. Stretching can be taught—we're trying to do that in this chapter—and yet it really has to be caught. You have to discover it by doing it. You may understand it in theory, but you're still a stranger until you go for it. Your first stretch might actually be learning how to stretch. Here are some suggestions to help you do it well.

- Interview someone you know who exemplifies a pattern of stretching. Consider asking them the following questions.

Listen for insights that will assist you as you continue your own stretching journey.

o Tell me about a time when you stretched yourself beyond your normal capacity. What were the short- and long-term results of the experience?

o Did you feel negative emotions during your stretching experience? Did you feel pain, frustration, or discouragement? When and why did you feel these emotions?

o Did you feel positive emotions during your stretching experience? Did you feel a sense of satisfaction, progress, or growth? When and why did you feel these emotions?

o What happened to your capacity as a result of your stretching experience? Did it stay the same? Did it grow? How could you tell?

• Think back on your life and identify a time when you really stretched yourself. Ask yourself the same questions. What can you learn about your stretching experience that might be helpful as you move forward?

• Consider each of the engagement drivers you've studied prior to this chapter and think through how the process of stretching could help you increase your capacity to implement those drivers in your life. Write down your answers to the following questions:

o In what ways might the other five drivers require me to stretch and go to my outer limits?

o What would the benefits be if I increased my capacity in certain areas (you choose which ones)?

• Conduct some personal research to increase your understanding of the following:

o The realities of stretching

o The benefits of stretching

o The lessons of stretching

• Discuss what you learned from this chapter with someone else. This discussion will be especially helpful if that person is also studying this chapter.

The Stretching Process

Step 1: Leave Your Comfort Zone
- Set specific goals
- Prioritize your goals
- Develop a plan
- Anticipate obstacles

Step 2: Pass Through Your Discomfort Zone
- Create momentum
- Recharge
- Enlist support
- Apply effective effort

Step 3: Go to Your Outer Limits
- Track progress
- Celebrate successes
- Recover from failure

Step 1: Leave Your Comfort Zone

If it's not clear by now, your comfort zone can be your danger zone. Staying there for any length of time is hazardous to your personal and professional health. You risk losing your competitiveness and your sense of self-worth. You probably know this from personal experience. Yet it takes a strong personal commitment to consistently pursue personal growth through stretching. So how do you do it?

Set Specific Goals

First, find your gaps and opportunities. Consider where you need to make improvements in your skills, knowledge, experience, and performance. Remember to look both ways. Look forward and identify areas where you want to build increased capacity based on your motivation and the organization's needs. But also look backward. Look for areas where you have demonstrated a pattern of weakness, where you're underdeveloped, where you fall short, lack confidence, or simply need to get better. Determine what it will take to improve in each area you want to improve. And don't forget to be specific and clear. A fuzzy stretch goal won't help you in the long run. For example, a fuzzy goal would be, "I want to become a better communicator." A more specific goal would be, "I want to become a better public speaker."

Prioritize Your Goals

You'll most likely find it helpful to keep a list of potential stretch goals based on the gaps and opportunities you've identified. As you add to your list, prioritize your goals each time. Don't take on everything at once. In fact, we normally recommend pursuing only two development goals at a time. To create a breakthrough in performance, you need to put a disproportionate amount of attention behind something. Having too many goals is like having no goals at all. It's the focus and concentration of resources that makes the difference.

To help you prioritize, think about each of your goals along two separate dimensions. First, think about the personal rewards that will come if you accomplish the goal. Second, consider the professional rewards that might come as well. Now think about the combined impact of achieving the goal with both dimensions in mind.

Figure 5.2 shows the relationship between personal and professional rewards, with three examples given on the graph. It's a helpful way of comparing your goals. Based on where you plot your goals, it often makes sense to start with the goal that is the highest on both dimensions because it's important and motivating at the same time. In this example, option A provides high personal rewards but low professional impact. Option B is just the opposite. Option C has high values on both dimensions. All things being equal, option C is the best choice. So put option C at the top of your list, at least for now.

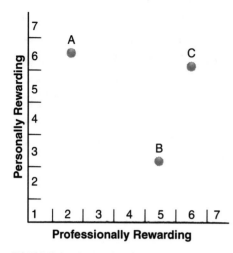

FIGURE 5.2   Comparing Personal and Professional Rewards

Develop a Plan

Goals without plans are mere wishes. If you don't have an action plan by the time you step into your discomfort zone, you'll most likely falter and then scurry right back to your comfort zone. An action plan can help you look beyond the challenges of the moment, knowing that there's a plan to see you through it all. You will also want to predict your discomfort barriers and define breakthrough strategies to help you survive the difficult times.

A solid plan will include a completion date for your goal. It also needs a simple schedule with milestones. A milestone is an accomplishment that marks progress along the way. For example, if you set a stretch goal to become a more effective public speaker, you would want to identify points of accomplishment you could work toward. Milestones might include making a presentation to your work team, becoming a member of a local public speakers group, completing a public speaking course, speaking at a regional conference, and, finally, speaking at a national conference. Each of these could be a milestone to achieve as you work to realize your ultimate stretch goal.

Anticipate Obstacles

Suppose options B and C in Figure 5.2 have a number of obstacles that would be very challenging to overcome, but option A has fewer and smaller obstacles. Consider going after option A first so you can get a quick win and build some momentum. But we're not quite done with our analysis.

Guidelines such as these can help you strike a balance between the rewards and the degree of difficulty. But there's no formula to give you the right answer of what goal to pursue. Sometimes, it makes sense to pick a harder goal because it's more important. Remember, you need stretch goals that challenge you, push you, and test you. If you intend to experience the full benefits of stretching, don't be afraid to take on a goal that's hard to reach. That's why it's called stretching.

Sometimes stretching is thrust upon us and we have no choice. But remember, we're talking about stretching by design. When you do, try not to leave your comfort zone unprepared. That's what scares people and convinces them that's it's better to stay safe in the comfort zone. For example, one barrier to the goal of becoming a better public speaker might be the sheer terror of standing in front of people. Or you may worry that you're going to start shaking or coughing, or simply freeze up. You may be worried that you don't have anything meaningful to say. There are a hundred different potential obstacles, but which ones bother you the most?

You've heard it said that starting is the hardest part. That's often true. One of the first obstacles you'll face is the dear old friend that we call inertia. Inertia is the gravity we feel that keeps us in our comfort zone. It's that tendency to remain in a state of rest and inactivity.

The Inertia Monster

In January, you can walk into any health club and greet the same scene: An hour wait for a spin bike. Aerobics classes spilling into the halls. Smiles, sweat, and heavy breathing. From gym to gym, it's the same story. There's high energy and shared motivation.

Two weeks later, the scene has changed: rows of idle elliptical machines, racks of stoic weights. And listen. What do you hear? The decibel reading has plummeted from 85 to 42. Give it one more month, and the annual burst followed by the desolate aftermath will be complete. A lot of things change over time, but the basic pattern of human behavior remains the same.

In most cases, a goal—in this case a New Year's resolution—is an act of violence against the status quo. It pits you against yourself. Self 1 wants to experience the exhilaration and rewards of pushing to your outer limits. Self 2 is firmly ensconced in the routines, stability, and equilibrium of life. Self 1 wants to disturb. Self 2 wants to preserve.

Self 1 feels the excitement, promise, and anticipation of a new year. There is an air of expectancy. Self 2 is resistant and content. But in the first days of the new year, Self 1 overpowers Self 2 with a sense of urgency and renewed hope.

Most New Year's resolutions are goals to achieve meaningful behavioral change. For example, exercise more, eat less, get out of debt, stop smoking, demonstrate more patience, become a better leader, and the like. These things are more than tweaks or tinkering at the margins.

Effecting behavioral change is astonishingly difficult. It pegs out at a 10 on a 10-point scale. If you have doubts, consider the avalanche of confirming data. Success is a deviant case. Studies show achievement rates for New Year's resolutions in the 10 percent to 20 percent range, so there's a high chance you will wake up one day before January has expired and realize that your resolutions have passed into history in the form of noble intent.

The pattern is one of early failure. We tend to flame out quickly because we rely on the shelf life of emotion. Emotion is a great catalyst for change, but it's more like a booster rocket. It gets you off the launching pad, but it won't sustain the journey.

Most people go slack after just a few days. The inertia monster stages a coup and rehoists the flag of the status quo, quashing the effort. We slump into intractable and rebellious complacency. We accept defeat quickly, run a soothing script in our minds, and resume normal patterns of behavior. And for all of this we have several perfectly logical explanations at the ready. Furthermore, it doesn't help that our mainstream culture is in a mad rush for on-demand thrills, sensations, and instant gratification. A long, hard slog to change behavior can be an exquisitely difficult journey.

Success is not the absence of failure. It's the rejection of a life of ease, which also happens to guarantee some failure. It's a willingness to travel to your outer limits. Go at it again, but this time put up some scaffolding for support. We often use what we call the "Eight Here-to-There Questions" to help leaders and organizations prepare for goal achievement.

1. Do I know what the goal is?
2. Do I know how to achieve the goal?
3. Do I have the resources to achieve the goal?
4. Do I have the skills to achieve the goal?
5. Can I measure the goal?
6. Am I accountable for the goal?
7. When will I achieve the goal?
8. How will I replenish energy along the way?

If you have good answers to all eight questions, you have a solid chance of sustaining your efforts far beyond the shelf life of emotion. Remember, the uncelebrated little things lead to the celebrated big things. Finally, listen to Self 1. Tell Self 2 to hit the gym.

Our advice is to expect the obstacles. Fully anticipate them. And count on some you didn't anticipate. There's a 100 percent chance you'll face some obstacles you didn't think of. If you try to identify them and prepare for them in advance, you'll have more confidence to meet them. Heavyweight boxer Mike Tyson once said, "Everyone has a plan until they get punched in the mouth." Fully expect to take some shots. One of the first things we can do is eliminate the need to be surprised when obstacles appear. For each potential obstacle, consider how you'll respond if and when it arrives. If one of your obstacles is a fear of speaking to people you don't know, find an opportunity to speak to people you do know. That will get you started.

> *"One does not discover new lands without first consent-ing to lose sight of the shore for a very long time."*
> André Gide, winner of Nobel Prize in literature

Step 2: Pass Through Your Discomfort Zone

How do you know when you're stretching? It begins with the first signs of discomfort. The discomfort zone is not your final desti-nation. Nor is it a rest stop. It's a place to pass through. You'll know you're a seasoned stretcher when you find yourself passing through your discomfort zone on a regular basis and you relish the challenges that lie ahead. Meanwhile, here are some suggestions to help you move through this step.

Create Momentum

The more discomfort you feel, the closer you are to your outer limits. Get there as soon as possible. How? Maintain momen-tum with small wins. It's vital that you anticipate and celebrate success at intervals. Small wins increase your confidence. They help you maintain your forward momentum as you push your way through the discomfort zone. Ultimately, small wins pro-vide a power that will sustain the effort required to get to your outer limits.

Recharge

Sometimes it helps to step away from the battle for a time to decompress and gather the strength you need to begin moving for-ward again. Even fish know this concept. There are certain rivers in the world that teem with upward-swimming salmon at spawn-ing time. In the heart of Perthshire, Scotland, there wends such a river. At the base of the Falls of Dochart, there's a deep pool where salmon, before moving upstream, instinctively rest before engaging in the strenuous effort of leaping their way up through the rushing waters of the falls. Dochart Falls presents a significant obstacle that could prove fatal without a well-timed rest.

Pausing to gather strength, or waiting for conditions to be right, is common practice for salmon. Radio tracking studies confirm this. At some point, the salmon rest in their journey to gather strength and then move on. They settle down and remain in a semidormant state, wisely conserving energy so they can navigate forward through the many obstacles that lie ahead. As you move forward in your stretching journey, you're well advised to do the same, with this caution: never pause because things are difficult; pause only when you need to gather energy. Finally, pause only long enough to gather the energy you need. Otherwise, the monster of inertia could persuade you to end your journey right there.

> *"Whether you think you can or can't, you're probably right."*
>
> Henry Ford, inventor of the assembly
> line for automobile manufacturing

Enlist Support

Share your stretch goals with family, friends, and trusted colleagues, and invite them to help you celebrate your wins along the way. Whenever possible, seek counsel from those who may have already stretched in your area of opportunity, or who may be stretching in similar areas. Whatever you do, don't let anyone deprive you of the full benefits of stretching. Well-meaning people may attempt to help you accomplish your stretch goal by minimizing the discomfort that naturally accompanies the stretching process. Out of jealousy or resentment, others will try to persuade you to stop.

Apply Effective Effort

Effective effort is the consistent, focused, and smart application of effort over time.[6] Your outer limits represent a place that you've never been before, at least not in this particular area. It's a great place to be. It's adventurous new territory. It's where good things happen.

> *"Ah, but a man's reach should exceed his grasp, or what's a heaven for?"*
>
> Robert Browning, poet

We once had an individual we took through an executive coaching process. He worked in a manufacturing company and was perceived as a high-potential employee. He asked us to help him identify what he needed to do to become an executive in the company. We interviewed many people in the organization who worked with him and knew him well. We asked them several questions, one of which was this: "What does this person have to do to become an executive?"

The feedback was unanimous. Every person we talked to felt this individual had tremendous technical skill. He also demonstrated impressive social skills and was willing to jump in and help with any project or responsibility. And he was willing to work late hours to get the work done. But there was one glaring weakness that also came to the surface. This individual didn't understand the business. And he didn't act interested in understanding the business. He stuck with what he knew from his past experience and wasn't adjusting well to broader responsibility.

When we gave him the feedback, he didn't resent it. Instead, he immediately set a goal to learn the business from stem to stern. He put in place a detailed plan. He left his comfort zone that day and began the stretching process. His plan included the equivalent of achieving a "mini MBA" in his company. With all of his day-to-day responsibilities, he came in early and stayed late to achieve his goal. He studied. He observed. He asked questions. He pushed his thinking. He made demands of himself that he hadn't made in the past. The organization didn't grant him special dispensation from his day job. He had to do it all.

How did it feel? He often felt vulnerable. He had to admit that he didn't understand some things—that he didn't have nearly as many answers as he thought he did. But over time, he got comfortable in the place of not knowing. He even gained confidence enough to ask his subordinates questions that he previously would not have asked. In the process, he became a more engaging, genuine, and humble individual. The stretching process not only increased his knowledge of the business, it also changed his approach to leadership. He started leading with questions rather than answers, and to his astonishment, he became a more effective leader. Why? Because he was making his people stretch in the process of his own stretching. Can you guess the result? He was promoted to an executive leadership position.

Step 3: Go to Your Outer Limits

Your destination is your outer limits. And we don't mean a brief visit or overnight stay. You have to spend some good time there. You don't have to live there, but you need enough time to take your performance to a new level. This is where the magic happens. Otherwise, the rubber band theory applies: you can stretch beyond your current capacity, but if you fail to build new capacity, you will spring back to where you started. In statistics, they call it reverting to the mean. Capacity is increased as you go to your outer limits and stay a while. Here are a few suggestions to help you through this final step.

Track Progress

As you sustain your stretch, it's important to measure your performance. If you're measuring sales revenue, that's easy. But if you're trying to measure your effectiveness in public speaking, that's hard. Even if you have to rely on qualitative data, use what you can.

Celebrate Successes

Acknowledge meaningful progress. But make sure that what you are celebrating is truly meaningful. Sometimes people manufacture celebrations in the hope that it will create motivation. We disagree. If it's not real, it has no real impact. But when you do hit a milestone or overcome a significant barrier, mark the occasion.

Recover from Failure

Some people call it bounce-backability, and it's one of the most important attributes that you can develop. You will have setbacks. There's no question about that. In fact, the bigger your goals, the more often you will fail. So you have an early choice: set common goals and succeed more often, or set uncommon goals and succeed less often. In any event, there will be failure unless you hibernate in your comfort zone. The real key to your success will be in your recovery, your response to setbacks. The way you respond when you fail is the greatest single predictor of long-term success. Success is not about your rate of success. It's about trying, failing some of the time, and succeeding some of the time. And hopefully, your rate of success increases as you learn to try more effectively.

> *"Success is how you bounce when you hit the bottom."*
> General George S. Patton

Both success and failure are temporary. Just replace the word *failure* with the word *learning*, and you get the point. Don't be afraid of learning, and don't be afraid of what people think. When it comes to stretching and failing forward, those who do it well are people who have developed a healthy ability to discount what detractors and naysayers might be saying. They're not rude or intolerant, but they have to be able to at least think, "Thank you for your advice, but your opinion doesn't count on this issue." This discounting ability is often critical to maintain the drive and motivation to persevere in the face of adversity.

Your Résumé of Failure

In my executive coaching practice, I (Tim Clark) do something unusual. Before I meet with the executive for the first time, I ask him or her to prepare a written résumé for me to review. When we get together in person, we review it, and then I ask the question, "Do you also have a résumé of failure?"

The response is usually a blank stare.

"What do you mean?"

"Well, your résumé is nice, but I need to know the history of your success. Much of that history is traceable to failure. So if you've never written your own résumé of failure (not a single executive has), I'd like to invite you to take that opportunity."

At this point, the executive gets nervous.

"Don't worry," I say. "I can promise you that it will be one of the most powerful exercises in self-examination that you've ever done. It's something to look forward to."

At this point, some of the executives look at me as if I'm crazy.

"Here's how it works. First, I want you to list and describe the top 10 most spectacular failures of your life—personal and professional. (I've learned that trying to separate personal and professional life is a waste of time. You need the whole picture.) I don't want 3. I want 10, because I want you to search diligently through your personal history. Often our failures become the most formative and defining experiences of our lives. I want to know what makes you you, and this is one of the most important ways to learn that.

"Second, I want you to explain what happened and why. Don't write a dissertation. A quick description will do. Give me some context. Help me understand a little background on each failure.

"Third, and this is the last step, tell me what you learned from and felt about each failure. I really want to know. No happy talk. No political spin. Don't pull any punches. I want to know the truth. We all have failures. Some of our failures are excruciatingly painful. They are crucibles.

"Here's my final point: Failure is not a tragedy. Not learning from failure is a tragedy. Quitting is a tragedy. You obviously haven't quit, so that is a tragedy we don't have to deal with. That leaves us with learning from failure. We have to escape the tragedy of not learning from it. I'm not suggesting you haven't learned from your failures. What I am suggesting, however, is that we often haven't learned all we could have. Often, we find that we haven't plumbed the depths of the failure experiences we've had. We didn't wring out every lesson. That's what I'm asking you to do now. I want you to write your résumé of failure, and I want you to be proud of it. You may resent me now for giving you this assignment, but I promise you'll thank me later."

Here's what happens: most of the executives I've worked with treasure their résumés of failure. When they complete the assignment, they step back in amazement. It's priceless to them. One of the more confident leaders I've worked with shows people his résumé of failure (I'm not necessarily suggesting that, by the way), and he will tell you very matter-of-factly that he's had some successes in life as well as some glorious failures. And then he goes on to point out the valuable lessons he's learned from his failures.

Now it's your turn. Use Table 5.1 to write your own résumé of failure. It's a simple exercise, and yet it's not simple at all. Not surprisingly, it's a stretch assignment. If you take it seriously, you'll be glad you did.

TABLE 5.1   Your Résumé of Failure

Name:
Step 1. List the 10 most spectacular failures of your life, both personal and professional.
1.
2.
3.

TABLE 5.1 Continued

Name:

4.

5.

6.

7.

8.

9.

10.

Step 2. Explain each failure. What happened and why?

1.

2.

3.

4.

5.

6.

7.

8.

9.

10

Step 3. What did you learn from each failure? How did you feel?

1.

2.

3.

4.

5.

6.

7.

8.

9.

10.

Sometimes in our personal and professional life, we have to hit the breaking point without breaking. We have to figure out a way to carry on. Most of the time, we discover that we have more capacity than we thought, but we simply needed a stretching experience to know that. At other times, we simply fail. It's not a bad thing to have some spectacular failures on your résumé.

When we fail forward, we become more honest with ourselves. We square up to our strengths and weaknesses. We even share them unabashedly with others because in the course of facing and overcoming challenges, we become more real, more genuine, and less motivated to impress people by showcasing only our successes. The best recovery from failure is the full and complete acknowledgment of it and the motivation to keep trying. It's incredibly refreshing to be around people who can do this.

> *"People think of us as a product of our successes. I'd actually argue that we're a product of the challenges we faced in life. And how we handled those challenges probably had more to do with what we accomplish in life."*
> John Chambers, CEO of Cisco Systems

Conclusion

We invite you to stretch, and in so doing, part ways with the patterns of the disengaged. Disengaged employees like to sit around and wait for the institutional machinery of the organization to carry them along. They end up doing a lot of waiting. Many disengaged people like it that way. They like their comfort zones. We all do to some extent, but in our hypercompetitive world, it's an unwise place to be.

Remaining in your comfort zone does harm to your motivation and puts you at risk professionally. Too much time in your comfort zone erodes capacity, limits performance, and decreases opportunity. Not least, it flatlines your engagement. No one achieves anything worthwhile without stretching. And you will never earn the right to make a contribution of any consequence if you're unwilling to stretch. Stretching unlocks your potential. It frees you from the tyranny of circumstance and the philosophy of victimhood.

If you're willing to stretch, professional life will be more adventurous, more successful, and more fun.

> *"The passion for stretching yourself and sticking to it, even (or especially) when it's not going well, is the hallmark of the growth mindset."*
> Carol Dweck, Stanford psychologist

Tips for Leaders

By definition, it's a leader's job to build capacity in people by stretching them. Here are several tips you can use as a leader to help your people stretch more successfully:

- ☐ Help your employees select professional development goals that allow them to stretch. Meet with them one-on-one to help set and review goals. Help them narrow the scope and focus on one or two goals at a time in order to make significant progress. Help them set the goals appropriately—not too high to demoralize, not too low to trivialize. Help them put plans in place to accomplish their stretch goals.
- ☐ Give stretch assignments to your employees. Match organizational priorities with the abilities and potential of your people. Be supportive but not directive, allowing the employee to create a plan to fulfill the assignment. Help your employees interpret and manage risk.
- ☐ Monitor your employees' progress throughout the year and make sure they're stretching. Invite them to engage in

frank coaching sessions to discuss progress. Offer help and guidance along the way.

☐ Help your employees anticipate, face, and overcome obstacles. These are the golden moments of influence when a leader can make a big difference in the life of an employee. Show empathy and yet teach and model resolve and persistence toward the goal.

☐ Celebrate your employees' successes. Show your people that their success is a measure of your success. Rejoice in their accomplishments.

☐ Model stretching by setting and sharing your own stretch goals. Become a living case study of a person who exemplifies the three-step stretching process.

☐ Set the parameters for failure. Ensure that everyone understands the tolerable limits of failure. Openly discuss the importance of failure and the margin for error that is acceptable. When someone fails forward, celebrate and communicate what was learned in the process.

☐ Use Table 5.2 to determine where your team members are in their readiness to begin the stretching process. Conduct an assessment of each direct report. This will be your baseline as you begin to work with your people. We suggest that you fill out the assessment for each individual and then have the individuals themselves do the same assessment. Have a dialogue and share your results with each other. This will provide a natural segue to the process of setting stretch goals.

TABLE 5.2   Assessment of Readiness to Begin the Stretching Process

Stretching Questions	1. To a very small extent	2. To a small extent	3. To a moderate extent	4. To a great extent	5. To a very great extent
1. I volunteer for stretch assignments when they are available.	O	O	O	O	O

TABLE 5.2 Continued

Stretching Questions	1. To a very small extent	2. To a small extent	3. To a moderate extent	4. To a great extent	5. To a very great extent
2. I demonstrate a consistent pattern of stretching.	O	O	O	O	O
3. I set stretch goals that are neither too high nor too low.	O	O	O	O	O
4. I consistently identify areas of professional development that are important to the success of the organization.	O	O	O	O	O
5. I create detailed plans to accomplish my stretch goals.	O	O	O	O	O
6. I manage the stress and risk of leaving my comfort zone and going to my outer limits.	O	O	O	O	O
7. I ask for help when I'm outside my comfort zone and I'm not performing well.	O	O	O	O	O
8. I demonstrate a pattern of failing forward: I learn from failure and keep trying.	O	O	O	O	O

TABLE 5.2   Continued

Stretching Questions	1. To a very small extent	2. To a small extent	3. To a moderate extent	4. To a great extent	5. To a very great extent
9. I track my progress and celebrate small successes when I'm working toward a stretch goal.	O	O	O	O	O
10. I have clear priorities to increase my capacity in one or more areas of my professional life.	O	O	O	O	O

6

Achieve: Jump into the Cycle!

"The value of achievement lies in the achieving."
Albert Einstein

What Is It About Achieving?

On May 26, 1953, two climbers that you've never heard of attempted to get to the summit of Mount Everest. They got within 300 feet (91 m) of the top and then had to turn back when their oxygen systems failed.

Three days later, Edmund Percival Hillary, a 33-year-old New Zealand mountaineer and explorer, and Sherpa mountaineer Tenzing Norgay made the same attempt and achieved their goal. They became the first climbers to reach the summit of the tallest point on earth. It practically took an army to support the two climbers who would ultimately stand on top of the world. It took no fewer than 400 people and 10,000 pounds of baggage and supplies to build a base camp. It also took two months to complete the feat. On the day that Hillary and Tenzing climbed to the top of Everest, snow and wind held them up at the South Col for two days. The morning of the ascent, Hillary discovered that his boots had frozen solid outside the tent. He spent two hours warming them before he and Tenzing set out with 30-pound (14-kg) packs to make the attempt.

The crucial stretch of the ascent was a 40-foot (12-m) rock face that later became known as the "Hillary Step." Hillary found a way to wedge his way up a crack in the face between the rock wall and the ice, and Tenzing followed. They reached Mount Everest's 29,029-foot (8,848-m) summit, the highest point on earth, at 11:30 a.m. As Hillary put it, "A few more whacks of the ice axe in the firm snow, and we stood on top." They stayed a mere 15 minutes at the summit before starting the arduous journey down. News of the successful expedition reached Britain on the day of the coronation of Queen Elizabeth II. Hillary was subsequently knighted by the new queen, and Tenzing received the British Empire Medal.

> *"People do not decide to become extraordinary. They decide to accomplish extraordinary things. It is not the mountain we conquer but ourselves."*
> Sir Edmund Percival Hillary, first man
> to summit Mount Everest

Here are the essential facts of the expedition.

Height of Mount Everest: 29,029 feet

Success rate of climbers: 1 in 10

The average time a climber spends on top of the world: 60 minutes

The average time a climber spends climbing Mount Everest: 2 months

The average time a climber spends preparing, planning, and training to climb Mount Everest: 12 months

Mountain climbing may not be your thing. But we all have mountains to climb. Yours may be finishing a project on schedule and under budget, designing a new product, improving an important process, or bringing a new team together. Regardless of the pursuit, achieving is very much the same. It's the process of focusing and sustaining your efforts to accomplish something meaningful.

Achieving is the process of focusing and sustaining your efforts to accomplish something meaningful.

We talked about the Mount Everest principle in the last chapter. When climbers approach the top, they enter the "death zone" where the wind blows 180 miles per hour and visibility is negligible. Of course, most achievements don't feature a death zone, but they do involve a journey with obstacles and setbacks. Mountain climbing helps us understand the process. The summit is the crowning achievement of the journey, but it's not just the summit that motivates us to climb. There are small victories along the way that provide momentum and a sense of forward progress. When the journey becomes a long, hard slog, think about what keeps you going. Often, it's the satisfaction of the progress you've made. In the end, achieving is a transformative process. A conversion takes place along the journey. When we come out on the other side, we're forever changed.

Everest is a big, bold example of achieving, and it's very instructive. But let's be realistic. Most of us will never attempt Everest. We're not daring mountaineers. We'll never get close to the Himalayas. It will forever be something we read about. Yet the principle of achieving is exactly the same regardless of the mountains we climb.

When my (Tim Clark) daughter was six years old, she started taking piano lessons. She's not the first to do that. The other kids have also taken piano lessons, and so I was excited to hear yet another child play "Camptown Races" 2,000 times. Gradually, my daughter learned the notes and could pluck out the melody with her right hand.

One day she came home from her piano lesson very unhappy. She informed my wife and me that her teacher would be holding a piano recital and that she would not be participating.

"Why not?" I asked.

"I'm not doing it, and no one can make me," she declared.

"But why?" I persisted.

"Because my fingers don't work, Dad," she said.

My wife and I smiled, nodded, and said we were very sorry to hear that. She would eventually come around, we thought. The weeks passed, and our daughter did learn the song but maintained her stance that she would not be participating in the recital. We played along up to the very day of the performance. She protested, but put her dress on and went with us. She said she was going to watch rather than play.

The moment finally came. The piano teacher announced my daughter's name. Nervously, she stood up and made her way to the stage. She perched herself on the edge of the bench with legs dangling six inches from the ground. From the other side of the concert hall, you wouldn't actually know that someone was sitting in front of the ebony, nine-foot concert grand piano.

She began plunking. Thirty seconds later she was done. She jumped down from the bench, made an awkward curtsy, and ran back to her chair. Before I could congratulate her, she pulled on my arm and whispered quietly, "Dad, Dad."

"Yes," I said.

"Dad, I want to do that again."

It may not have been the summit of Everest, but the little girl that went to that recital was not the same little girl that came home. That white-knuckle experience changed her. So it is with achievement.

Why Achieve?

Peter Drucker, a leading management guru, had an experience as a young man in Hamburg, Germany, that taught him a profound lesson in achieving. He went to hear the opera *Falstaff*, written by the nineteenth-century composer Giuseppe Verdi, which has since become one of the most popular operas. The performance left Drucker spellbound. He was so taken by the experience that he decided he needed to know more about the composer. What he found surprised him even more.

He learned that Verdi was 80 years of age when he wrote *Falstaff*. How could this be? And why would Verdi, who in his own lifetime was considered one of the greatest composers of the century, go to the effort of writing one more opera? It didn't seem to make sense. Why wouldn't he just bask in the glow of his fame and live out his remaining days in luxury and leisure? Then came the answer: "All my life as a musician," wrote Verdi, "I have striven for perfection. It has always eluded me. I surely had an obligation to make one more try."[1]

What is it that motivates people to achieve? Why do some people continue striving and producing while others seem to coast or check out? When human beings achieve, for many obvious reasons, they become more engaged. The achievement cycle is self-renewing. Unlike a battery that needs to be replaced or recharged after use, achieving contains its own regenerative powers. Of course we don't always achieve when we set out to achieve. We have our failures, and those failures can be useful. At the same time, we can't fail all of the time or we would never try anything. We must reach the summit sometimes.

> "*I can charge a person's battery, and then recharge it, and recharge it again. But it is only when one has a generator of one's own that we can talk about motivation. One then needs no outside stimulation. One wants to do it.*"
>
> Frederick Herzberg

In fact, the achieving driver is linked in important ways to the other five drivers. The first and most obvious connection is between achieving and stretching. The two drivers are close cousins. Achieving means that you complete the entire cycle and accomplish the goal. If we stretch and don't achieve, we eventually stop stretching. Over time, stretching without achievement leads to burnout, disillusionment, and lower confidence.

Plus, you can't contribute much if you're not achieving at some level. Achieving removes barriers to shaping, provides meaning and purpose to learning, and sustains connecting. We could go on with other connections among the six drivers. The bottom line is that those who fail to maintain a pattern of achievement tend to put less effort into the other drivers. They become reluctant to shape. Their connections grow stale. Learning stagnates, and they lose the will to stretch.

We've made the claim that achieving brings its own rewards. What rewards? Let's be specific. First, let's start with the intrinsic rewards, the compensation that comes from the inside. When you achieve, you can have every expectation that you'll gain four specific internal rewards, or what we call the "four compensations." Achievement does the following:

1. **Replenishes energy.** We become recharged and renewed as we exert ourselves in the service of a worthy goal.
2. **Boosts confidence.** The actions we take lead to success, which reinforces our behavior, placing us in a virtuous achievement cycle. We have more belief that we can do it the next time.
3. **Increases capacity.** We take our knowledge and skill to another level every time we achieve something (as Tim's daughter did).
4. **Deepens fulfillment.** We feel better about ourselves for putting forth effort and exercising the discipline to follow through when we had every opportunity to quit.

"Our business in life is not to get ahead of others, but to get ahead of ourselves—to break our own records, to outstrip our yesterday by our today, to do our work with more force than ever before."

Stewart B. Johnson

From the inside out, these rewards keep us going mentally, emotionally, and physically. You can see why achieving is a driver of engagement. But there's another set of rewards that come from the outside, based on your relationship with the organization and its people. When you achieve something meaningful, especially when it benefits the organization, the organization normally sits up and takes notice. It often responds to that achievement and says, "Hey, look what this person did! We need to do something about that." In responding to the achievements of their members, organizations normally provide three forms of compensation:

1. **Recognition.** Organizations give public praise, approval, and commendation to people as a consequence of that achievement. They may acknowledge them in front of their peers to express appreciation. Recognition is usually something that we value. It makes us feel more valued and appreciated.

2. **Rewards.** Organizations give economic and noneconomic rewards to people as a consequence of achievement. It's another way for the organization to say, "We value what you have done, and we want to reciprocate." It could be anything from a raise to giving you the pick of the next project you're going to work on. Rewards can be big or small. In most cases, we appreciate them, and they help us feel more engaged.

3. **Responsibility.** When the organization learns that you have achieved something meaningful, especially if you have demonstrated a pattern of achieving great results, its leaders might say, "You know this person demonstrates a pattern

of achievement; let's give this person more responsibility." Increased responsibility often translates into more authority, influence, and control over resources and increased leadership participation, whether formal or informal.

"Without continual growth and progress, such words as improvement, achievement, and success have no meaning."

Benjamin Franklin

Because achieving is so demanding, most people need a mixture of internal and external rewards to make it worth the effort and sacrifice. We acknowledge both as important, but what about those times when the external rewards simply aren't there? What if the economy has dipped into a downturn? What if your company is losing money or being acquired? What if you've had four bosses in the last year? What if the company suddenly discontinues your product line and sends you back to a job you had five years ago? We can think of a thousand different scenarios in which the external rewards simply dry up or go away. What then?

The simple and right answer is that you go without. Sure enough, that's exactly what highly engaged employees do. They realize that sometimes the organization is going to have resources, and it's going to recognize and reward them. But other times, it won't, or it can't. Highly engaged employees know this. They stay mentally and emotionally prepared to press forward without those forms of compensation. The alternative is to play it safe and opt out of achievement due to the risk. As the great hockey player Wayne Gretsky once said, "You miss 100 percent of the shots you don't take." Whereas the highly engaged employee has a very different approach. She jumps right in. She does it for the organization, and she does it for herself. It's her career, her development, and her life. If you suppress your motivation to achieve, you ultimately hurt yourself. You stagnate, and your skills start to slip.

In a classic study conducted by Frederick Herzberg in the late 1960s, he asked essentially the same question Peter Drucker posed about Verdi: "Why did he write the opera?" In other words, what motivates people to go the extra mile, to give a little more, to go above and beyond? The number one factor was the motivation to achieve. After that came other motivations, such as "recognition, the work itself, responsibility, advancement, and growth."[2]

> *"Find courage to do something you are not ready to do."*
> Marissa Mayer, vice president, Google

Becoming an Achiever

It's not a neutral event when we don't achieve. There are real consequences. The most important consequence is that we live without the achievement and the compensation that would have come with it. What we forfeit is the opportunity cost of not achieving. When we contemplate jumping into the achievement cycle, we naturally think about the potential rewards. We ponder the costs, the risks, and the potential disappointments. We may not want to get up on that piano bench in front of the audience. Before you talk yourself out of anything, however, recognize that you can learn to become a better achiever. You don't have to accept your past performance as a measure of your future performance. Here are some suggestions for becoming a better achiever.

This Isn't Therapy

Don't wait for the organization to figure out your motivators. Some people believe it's the responsibility of the organization to understand them well enough to know what makes them tick and then provide just the right incentives to motivate them properly. This Pavlovian notion is silly. Yes, it's good for leaders to be empathetic, but an organization can't possibly develop the sensibilities to understand the deep psychology of every individual. You'll have to wait a millennium for that. Highly engaged people move forward in the meantime.

You Can Have Too Many Belt Buckles

We have a cowboy friend who competes in rodeo events. Whenever he wins an event, he brings home a huge cowboy belt buckle. We're not quite sure why anyone would want to wear such a piece of hardware, but make no mistake, these are highly coveted items. Napoleon said, "A soldier will fight long and hard for a bit of colored ribbon." Cowboys will fight even harder for one of these garish belt buckles. This raises some questions: What if there's no belt buckle or ribbon? What if there's no winner's purse? Are people still as motivated? Where does the stronger motivation come from? What kind of rewards fuel motivation for the long term?

One study concluded, "Careful consideration of reward effects reported in 128 experiments lead to the conclusion that tangible rewards tend to have a substantially negative effect on intrinsic motivation."[3] Another study concluded, "Rewards can deliver a short-term boost—just as a jolt of caffeine can keep you cranking for a few more hours. But the effect wears off—and, worse, can reduce a person's longer-term motivation to continue the project."[4] There is a large body of research that highlights the short shelf life of external motivation. In the past, we've often believed that rewards motivate, so we assumed that more rewards motivate more. Not true. There's a steep curve of diminishing returns where people hit a saturation point and more rewards produce almost no return. Because we're talking about sustainable engagement over the long term, external motivators should be used in conjunction with intrinsic motivators. A few cowboy belt buckles might be a good thing. But at some point, you just put them in the drawer. You have enough belt buckles to last a lifetime.

People Change

A person's motivation can change over time. One woman we studied said she was highly motivated to seek recognition and responsibility early in her career, but now she was more interested in the organization being responsive to her needs and preferences. Her motivation had changed based on her circumstances and stage of life. This could happen to you as well. As we move through different stages of life, our needs and preferences change. So too do our motivations to achieve. Your motivation to achieve is not cast in concrete. It's dynamic. Expect it to change.

Overachievement Can Be a Sickness

The motivation to achieve should not be confused with the high-need-for-achievement pathology that is an unhealthy addiction in some people. For people afflicted with this malady, achievement doesn't bring the normal rewards. Rather, it brings "relief in the accomplishment of tasks. Moving immediately to the next task on the list, they never savor accomplishments for long. This creates a vicious cycle marked by a feeling of little or no real sense of purpose and 'flatness'—in career and life."[5] This negative cycle is based on achieving for the wrong reasons, and it results in a serious imbalance.

In some cases, achievement can become a profoundly selfish activity, driven by ego or insecurity, in which people obsess on building a résumé of accomplishments as a sole means of showcasing themselves. In this case as well, the motivation is off the mark. We don't advocate anything like that. It only leads to cynicism and disengagement. We do believe that achievement is a moral obligation, that people have a responsibility to develop their potential and use their gifts to help and lift others. Idleness is dangerous, and the pursuit of pleasure can quickly become meaningless. At some point, our ability to contribute to others is based on the cultivation of our talents. Achievement brings greater depth and breadth to our offerings.

Entitlement Is Dangerous

The chalkboard aphorism reads, "If you want what you have never had, you must do what you have never done." One of the things that concerns us the most is the latest strain of entitlement that we see in society, in which people prefer leisure to performance and security to risk taking, "as if having enough money to satisfy one's desires were a human right rather than something to be earned."[6] Entitlement is the beguilement of low expectations. It's the treachery of believing you can violate the principle of work to achieve something worthwhile. It is the irony of claiming unqualified rights to things as the environment becomes more intensely competitive. These ideas are imitations of the real principle of achievement. They are inversions of truth.

Another common masquerade for genuine achievement is to rely on connections and credentials instead of competence, character, and real effort. If you're less willing to sacrifice, you're easily seduced with alternative routes to success. This kind of blinkered thinking eventually leads to ethical misconduct. It's easier to grease a palm or enter an unholy alliance than to get out there and sweat your way to a goal. When the seed of entitlement grows, it begins to crowd out initiative and healthy ambition. You start to tell yourself that effort really isn't the source of success. You go looking for substitutes.

Calvin Coolidge said it well: "Nothing in the world can take the place of persistence. Talent will not; nothing is more common than unsuccessful individuals with talent. Genius will not; unrewarded genius is almost a proverb. Education will not; the world is full of educated derelicts. Persistence and determination alone are omnipotent."

Don't Confuse Achievement with Pleasure and Accumulation

Achieving is the process of accomplishing versus accumulating, completing versus competing, improving versus stagnating, developing versus atrophying. With rampant commercialism, many of the marketing messages we hear are campaigns that promote indulgence and unbridled consumption instead of achievement. For example, in the popular teen movie *High School Musical 2*, a song entitled "Fabulous" portrays a self-absorbed rich kid singing, "I want it all." While the tune is catchy, the spurious message focuses on having things versus accomplishing things. Seeking pleasure to escape the climb of achieving is fool's gold. In the end it's a cheap imitation.

At dinner one night with a new client in the pharmaceutical industry, the conversation turned to Millennials in the workforce. Our client had just come from a focus group with new hires in their first jobs out of college. The feedback was alarming. The group of analytical hotshots told him they didn't want to do the analytical work that they were hired to do. Instead, they wanted more high-profile projects to work on, along with bigger salaries and bigger offices.

If we're not careful, we may fall for the doctrine of deserving things like these new hires. We may want to chase status without earning it. The highly engaged monitor their motives to understand if they are achieving in order to learn, develop, stretch, or contribute, or if they are achieving in order to accumulate and consume. Then they take steps to inoculate themselves against the harmful messages of commercialism and materialism. Pleasure and accumulation are not substitutes for solid and meaningful achievement. If we're not careful, they can lead to unrestrained grandiosity.

As one example, see Table 6.1 for an example of what happens when highly capable people confuse accumulation with achievement.

Confidence Is Drip-Fed

Why do people pass up an opportunity to achieve? There are lots of reasons, but one of the biggest is that they simply don't believe they can do it. They lack confidence. It's certainly rational to avoid trying to do something you can't do in order to conserve time and effort and avoid frustration and discouragement. The problem is

TABLE 6.1   Super Yacht Bragging Rights

Individual	Year	Yacht Length (Feet)	Yacht Name
Paul Allen	2000	303	*Tatoosh*
Roman Abramovich	2000	370	*Le Grand Bleu*
Paul Allen	2003	414	*Octopus*
Larry Ellison	2004	454	*Rising Sun*
Roman Abramovich	2010	557	*Eclipse*

Source: "The Billionaire with the Biggest Yacht Wins," *Bloomberg Businessweek,* August 4–14, 2011, 85.

that we don't really know if we can do things before we try. We have to catch ourselves when we start sounding like Eeyore saying, "End of the road . . . nothing to do . . . and no hope of things getting better. Sounds like Saturday night at my house." A lack of confidence leads to wrong thinking, inaction, and ultimately disengagement—not the achieving path you are looking for.

The process of achievement consists of hundreds, even thousands, of success moments linked together in a strand of satisfaction. Yet for some, the fear of failure keeps them on the couch. The only way to gain confidence is to gather the courage to take action. For instance, what's the most harmful thing a depressed person can do? Answer: nothing. Both the action and the achievement to which it leads are spiritual necessities.

Confidence is a drip-fed process. You can talk about it all you want, but you can't actually get confidence until you take the risk of venturing forth into the unknown. Norman Vincent Peale said, "Action is a great restorer and builder of confidence. Inaction is not only the result, but the cause of fear. Perhaps the action you take will be successful; perhaps different actions or adjustments will have to follow. But any action is better than no action at all."

> *"It is hard to fail, but it is worse never to have tried to succeed."*
>
> Theodore Roosevelt

Not Everybody's a Winner

You've heard the feel-good affirmation "Everybody's a winner." It feels good, but it requires nothing. In our culture we often start this therapy early. We have trophies for all the kids regardless of the win/loss record. That may be relatively benign, but what happens when this philosophy seeps into the cultural soil?

Albus Dumbledore, headmaster of Hogwarts, tells his star pupil, "It is our choices, Harry, that show what we truly are." That's a lesson we seem to be forgetting in American society. Rather than talk about choice and accountability, we want to talk about what we're entitled to. We want to talk about social injustice, the concentration of wealth, and corporate greed. It's true that our political and business leaders have abdicated their leadership responsibilities in many ways. But let's not excuse ourselves.

Winning is part of achieving. If we're not achieving, we're not winning. Winning starts when we look in the mirror. Let's be completely honest about our own behavior before we start fixing blame on some contextual factor, such as our boss, the organization, the economy, our small cubicle, or our lack of resources.

"In an information age," Joseph Nye Jr. writes, "communications become more important, and outcomes are shaped not merely by whose army wins but also by whose story wins." I'm afraid we've been telling ourselves the "everybody's a winner" story long enough that we're starting to believe it. It's a seductive piece of propaganda. It's a fraudulent brochure of personal achievement. It's a down payment on failure.

Think about what this crowd-pleasing doctrine does. It provides psychological relief for personal failure. It's a way to self-medicate. We're building an empire of superstition when we walk around repeating it. The truth is, a lot of people are not winning, so let's not imply the moral equivalence of everyone's behavior by repeating this slogan that negates choice and achievement. Human beings are consummately precious. They are winners in the sense that they have inherent worth. But achieving is a choice, and some people choose not to achieve.

Learn to Achieve

Cabdrivers in London have to pass a difficult exam in order to obtain a driver's license. It takes two to four years to become fully competent. They learn all the streets, attractions, fast routes, and even odd things like which houses have doorbells. They even remember the color of front doors. Studies have shown that as they achieve a level of proficiency in their profession, their brains become larger in some areas than other people's brains. And the longer they stay in the profession, the larger this specific part of their brain becomes.[7] Achieving is something you learn. Once you learn it, you grow accustomed to it. Once you grow accustomed to it, you expect it. It's no longer a surprise. When achieving becomes familiar, it can actually become a habit.[8]

> *"Life is change. Growth is optional. Choose wisely."*
> Karen Kaiser Clark

The Achievement Cycle

The regenerative powers of achieving are real. The best evidence of this is that people who learn to achieve continue to achieve. They learn the process and the behavior that lead to achievement. It's something anyone can learn. It's a simple process to learn, though not a simple process to do. But if you have the road map, it helps you understand the journey. All of the steps in the journey represent an achievement cycle that reinforces itself (Figure 6.1). The person who achieves is motivated to do it again, to go on another journey and achieve something else.

Step 1: Find a Mountain

The first step in the achievement cycle is to find a mountain. In other words, have a goal. People don't normally fall into achievement. They begin with a well-thought-out goal.

FIGURE 6.1   The Achievement Cycle

Having a Goal Creates Motivation

In 2011, after several years in the achievement cycle, Austrian mountaineer Gerlinde Kaltenbrunner became the first woman in the world to successfully climb all 14 peaks over 8,000 meters without the use of supplemental oxygen. After climbing K2, the second tallest mountain in the world and one of the most dangerous peaks, she said, "I visualized myself taking last few steps towards the peak." Gerlinde failed multiple times to summit K2, but the power of the goal kept her on track. From her example we learn an important principle: the act of setting a goal creates motivation to achieve it. Once you find a mountain, you set in motion cognitive, emotional, and physical processes. These processes immediately start working in the service of the goal.

Take a moment to think about the different mountains you might want to climb. Ask yourself the following questions:

- What are some of your aspirations?
- What are some of your gaps?

- What are your biggest challenges?
- What are your biggest worries?
- What do you need to do differently?
- What's holding you back from the next level of performance?
- What stories are you telling yourself to justify staying where you are? Do you buy the stories?

Ironically, sometimes in life we lose sight of our direction and we redouble our efforts. It doesn't get us very far. You have to start with a mountain to climb.

Strike a Balance Between Audacious and Realistic

The goal can be big or small. Our advice on goal setting is to strike a proper balance. Your goal should make you stretch, but it shouldn't be unachievable. There's a lot of advice out there on goal setting, and we've come to the conclusion that one size doesn't fit all. Sometimes it makes sense to set a seemingly impossible goal because it forces you to think and behave differently. It challenges your assumptions and paradigms. At other times, that kind of audacity is nothing but discouraging. The amount of stretch you put into your goal should be based on resources, circumstances, and constraints.

As you find a mountain to climb, ask yourself if your goal is really your goal or a decoy. Do you really want to climb this particular mountain, or do you just want to get yourself unstuck and move to a better place? Both approaches have merit. On balance, we still prefer the old-fashioned idea of setting a stretch goal and achieving it.

Don't Fall for Gimmicks

If there's one true principle the television program *The Biggest Loser* teaches, it's that we need to stop believing in the seven-day rapid fat loss promise and all the other specious claims in our society. If you've watched the program, it's clear there's no royal road to losing 100 pounds. Eat less, exercise more. Period. Translation: if you find a big mountain and think you can climb it in a day, you're probably mistaken. A mountain is a mountain. Respect the price of achievement. Any significant goal has a price tag that reflects its value. Don't try to convince yourself you can get something for nothing.

What Keeps Your Boss up at Night?

If you want to set a goal that really adds value to the organization, ask yourself what keeps your boss up at night. This simple question will give you a different perspective. It will infuse within you a sense of stewardship. If you can learn to set and achieve goals that allow your boss to sleep better, you will make yourself even more valuable.

> *"When you go into a day that's unplanned, then you're just faced with whatever hits you. If you have a plan, then you don't let the unplanned things get in your way."*
>
> David Besio

Step 2: Plan the Journey

Let's go back to the Mount Everest example. You don't just show up at the Everest North Base Camp in Tibet and start climbing. You'll never make it. You have to chart your course. You have to plan the journey. Good execution is based on careful, detailed planning, complete with a schedule, milestones, and contingencies. It means figuring out what to do and when, whether in sequence or in parallel. Perhaps it has an antique ring to it, but planning is the best way to manage risk and avoid failure. We once heard a member of Gen Y say, "I'm better on accident." It's kind of a hip thing to say. It's not a hip thing to do. Planning is a process that runs from general to specific. By the time you're done choosing a path, your preparation will become your greatest source of confidence.

In 1951, legendary science fiction writer Arthur C. Clarke published a short story titled "Superiority." The narrative explains how a superior galactic force is soundly defeated by an inferior one.

In years past, the story was required reading at the U.S. Military Academy at West Point because of its insight. Clarke writes, "With stubborn conservatism and complete lack of imagination, the enemy continued to advance with his old-fashioned and inefficient but now vastly more numerous ships."[8] Why? Good old-fashioned planning and solid execution. An awesome goal on one side won't beat an awesome plan on the other.

Sometimes we hastily assume that we have the wrong goal when the problem is a poor plan. Do you have the time, resources, and ability to achieve the goal? Do you know your margin for error in achieving the goal? What's the chance that you might be "crippled by your own science," as Clarke writes, because you think your aspiration alone will take you there?

Step 3: Move Your Feet

The third step in the achievement cycle is simply to move your feet. You've set up base camp, and you have a plan. It's time to move. The key to moving your feet is to create small victories along the way. Each small victory will give you momentum, confidence, and energy to keep going. If you can put a string of small victories together, they eventually add up to a big victory. The art of the small victory is the art of achieving.

During my first week at Oxford University, I (Tim Clark) attended a meeting for all of the new graduate students. Here I was in the middle of this medieval town, wearing a black robe, swearing oaths in Latin. As far as I was concerned, I felt as if I were attending Hogwarts.

I'll never forget what the professor said next. He told us to say hello to the person on our left and then to the person on our right. Then, after a long pause, he said, "You are all here to earn a doctorate degree from Oxford University. The truth is that only one out of three of you will achieve this. The other two-thirds of you will fail or quit." And then with great irony and a smile on his face, he said, "Welcome to Oxford."

Needless to say, I sat there in stunned silence. I knew that I was no genius. Now I seriously wondered if I was in the right place. The doubts started to creep in. "You may as well pack your bags and go home," I thought. "You can't cut it here."

Well, I stayed. I said to myself, "I'm just going to try." What I learned in the process was to look for and achieve the small victory, and then go the next one. One day of study, one assignment, one test at a time. I knew that I wasn't the smartest person in the room, so to speak, but I had this simple strategy to plod along, to move my feet and go from small victory to small victory.

When I achieved a small victory, it would energize me, and I'd make a little celebration. I might go to my favorite pub and get some fish and chips or take in a soccer game. It renewed my resolve and motivation to keep going. Every small victory boosted my confidence to do it again, to keep going. These were little achievement cycles that were invisible to the outside world. Well, guess what? After a few years of hard work, and quite honestly some failures along the way, all of those small victories added up to a big victory.

I woke up one morning, put on a red and blue robe, walked into the famous Sheldonian Theatre, and bowed before the Chancellor, who conferred on me the doctor's degree that I hadn't been quite sure I could ever achieve.

A small victory allows you to reenergize and move through a series of mini achievement cycles. Once you find a mountain and plan your journey, we recommend that you have three to five small victory goals in your back pocket. That's enough to get you started. It will help you keep moving your feet, and then you can come up with more as you move along. Here's your task: define at least three small victories in Table 6.2 that will help you accomplish one of your professional goals. Remember,

TABLE 6.2   Your Small Victory Goals

Small Victory 1
Small Victory 2
Small Victory 3
Small Victory 4
Small Victory 5

small victories deliver rewards in smaller doses. To guide you in the process, keep in mind that small victories have the following characteristics:

- **Short-term.** It's something you can accomplish in a short period of time.
- **Visible or measurable.** It's tangible evidence that you have done something that matters, that you have made progress and gained forward motion.
- **Aligned with the bigger goal.** There's a clear connection to what's important to the organization and to you personally and professionally.

> *"If man would move the world, he must first move himself."*
>
> Socrates

You have your mountain. You have your plan. Now it's time to move. You've transitioned from the stage of preparation to the stage of action. It's go time. Actually moving your feet and achieving the small victories one after another is more a matter of personal discipline than anything else. There's nothing too fancy about it. It's about will and determination, and it requires focus and the elimination of distractions. At this point, the way you manage and allocate your time becomes a critical success factor.

Don't Be a Time-Management Junk Dealer

I've (Tim Clark) learned that to really achieve, you can't just be a visionary at 30,000 feet. You also have to be a great tactician on the ground. If you want the small victories, you have to be effective in executing your plan every day, and that comes down to time management.

I walked into an office once that resembled a slot canyon. When I crossed the threshold, I had to turn sideways and sidestep my way through a narrow corridor between two walls of stuff in order to find my way to a little foldout chair. I expected to see Redd Foxx, who played a junk dealer in the '70s sitcom *Sanford and Son.*

The problem with junk dealers is that they don't know how to assign value to what they have. It's all treasure—in which case, it's all junk. There's no treasure in the world save for its relationship to nontreasure. But if you don't know the difference, you'll find yourself swimming in junk. Consider that a vintage 1932 L.C. Smith Corona model 4 typewriter is worth about $800. My Dell OptiPlex 755 from 2007 is worth about 8 cents.

The same principle holds true for time management and the ability to achieve. There are time-management junk dealers. They trade their time for almost any unit of work or pleasure. Real collectors, on the other hand, trade their time only for those of high value. When it comes to time management, ask yourself if you deal in junk or in real collectibles.

Great achievement is based on great time management. It's a learned behavior and not a widely distributed behavior. Here's what it looks like in part.

Prioritize Till It Hurts

Hold your breath. The greatest time management invention is—that's right, the list. You can use a yellow pad or a smartphone app. It doesn't matter that much. Just make sure you document your priorities and manage them dynamically. Behaviorally, the best time managers observe a daily ritual in which they add tasks and refresh their priority list every day without fail. They also do weekly planning, midrange planning, and long-term planning. The magic is not in the tool or the process, however. It's in the execution. Someone said the definition of success is doing the task at hand well. What's the task at hand? That's the less obvious question and the day-in-and-day-out hard thing to do. It's the grinding discipline of wringing out your priorities. Time is your scarce resource. Don't trade it for junk.

Avoid Meaningless Units of Pleasure

When it comes to trading time for units of pleasure, it's fascinating that almost all of the world-class time managers I know rarely, if at all, trade time for prime-time television, web surfing, or video gaming. Their media consumption habits are sparing. Junk dealers browse the menu of offerings. Collectors know what they want before they shop. Go for quality, not kitsch.

Don't Get Hijacked

Hijacking your time is the special talent of media and technology in the digital age. If you sat down at your desk this morning and got sucked into the vortex of a long, unplanned e-mail session, you know what I'm talking about. Remind yourself that you're the one who trades your time. Don't let devices or people allocate it for you. You're the sovereign of your seconds and the master of your minutes.

Remember the One-Touch Rule

We spend a lot of time approaching, circling, sniffing, kicking, tasting, and simply thinking about tasks without doing them. We check on them like a babysitter to see if they're still sleeping. We pat their heads and then walk away, only to come back later. To this day, I've never seen a task jump out of the crib and get itself done. Tasks sleep eternally until we wake them. If you touch a task, complete the task.

Manage Walk-in Traffic

The triage of time management says some things are important; some things are not. Some things are urgent; some things are not. Focus on what's important and urgent first, and what's important second. Leave the rest alone. That makes sense, but on the ground it can be difficult when the urgent tasks come calling. Walk-in traffic can foil any good plan.

Great time managers communicate their time constraints up front when people walk in. They're not rude and curt—they're clear and kind. If it turns out to be important, be flexible and spend the time. If it's not, acknowledge the person but don't trade time for junk when there's treasure ahead.

Step 4: Adjust and Adapt

The third step in the achievement cycle is to adjust and adapt. On the mountain, the weather changes, the temperature drops, and the sun goes down. In organizations, it's the same. You may have the best plan ever put together, but you still can't forecast an unplanned event. On one occasion, British Prime Minister Harold Macmillan was asked what his greatest challenge was. He responded, "Events, my dear boy, events." Unforeseen events will be part of the journey.

To adjust and adapt effectively requires what we call *turbulence capacity*. It's the ability to adapt to the speed and volatility of the competitive environment. On a personal level, it's the ability to face your fears, weaknesses, and shortcomings when they're being tested. In the world of organizations, it's vital that you develop this capacity to adjust in today's unpredictable environment. If you crave security, constancy, and equilibrium, you'll probably fall off the mountain when the first storm rolls in.

In a recent interview, the author Sylvia Nasar said, "From the beginning of civilization to the nineteenth century, 90 percent of humanity was stuck in place, even if their country did comparatively well. Average people lived like livestock—they didn't go anywhere, read anything, or wear much; they ate bad food and didn't live a very long time."[9]

We wouldn't trade centuries with those people, but at least they took some comfort in the familiar. Today, we live in a near-constant state of disturbance. We're anything but stuck in place, and it poses an unprecedented challenge for leaders. Leadership has become a more dangerous calling. The principles haven't changed, but the conditions have.

The tenor of the times is different. The atmospheric pressure of competition continues to rise, and not just in business. It's the same in education, government, healthcare, and the nonprofit sector. It used to be that you could spend a good deal of your career traveling across plains and prairie where the landscape was relatively flat and wide open. Now we've all come to a mountainous, craggy expanse.

Your ability to adjust and adapt has become a threshold requirement in the global age. It requires two things: the performance of work and the absorption of stress. Even the hale and hearty will encounter the "death zone" at certain points in the journey. To achieve in the twenty-first century requires a deep psychological acceptance of the existing turbulence.

Until then, we can find ourselves engaged in a personal battle of denial against the new normal, its pace and its dynamism. If you feel yourself slipping into patterns of resistance, resignation, or political expediency, ask yourself what year it is. That tends to help. We're not saying that your career will be one transformational epoch after another. No matter how anticipatory you try to be, there will be blindsiding threats that appear without warning. There will be killer applications and disruptive technologies. We can't divine where the next challenge will come from, but we do know it will come. It's hard to "Keep your fears to yourself, but share your courage with others," as Robert Louis Stevenson once enjoined. It's hard to look the future in the face. It's uncharted, unscripted, and unknown. And yet we're galloping in that direction.

Step 5: Summit

The final step in the achievement cycle is to summit. When you're ready to summit, however, you're not fresh and energetic. You're tired, but you're not done. And there's still a host of distractions, temptations, and obstacles to overcome. On balance, humans are brilliant starters. They are poor finishers.

Finding a mountain to climb is the easy part. It's easy to start exercising. It's easy to enroll in school. It's easy to hatch a new business idea. It's easy to be nice, refrain from cursing, serve others, or listen to your spouse—that is, for a day. It's less easy on the second day. The grade gets steeper, and it doesn't change until you're at the summit. If you've started a half-pound cheeseburger, don't worry about going the distance. But if you've started a new job, a new project, or a new skill, hang in there.

As you might expect, the study of personal achievement is more often the study of failure. Positive achievement represents positive deviance. If you're a serious student of achievement, you can expect to spend most of your time sifting through the wreckage of things that started well and ended poorly. People and the organizations they create are littered with the failed remains of false starts.

But in the wreckage, we find critical insights. One of the biggest is that we simply take our hands off the wheel too soon. We get tired. We get bored. We get distracted. And then we fail. It happens over and over. Sometimes we learn from our failures. But it usually takes a while to really dial in the desire and the discipline to be a finisher and go to the summit.

The last step of achievement—the act of summiting—comes from the inside. When the lights go down and the cheering crowds disperse, you're on your own. And that's usually what summiting is all about. It's lonely, inglorious work. If you feed on praise and recognition, summiting is hard. Why finish the job when you can seek out a new company and go to the next gig?

Think about summiting in organizations. Think about the perverse incentives that tempt us to throw in the towel prematurely. Starting is for the rock star. This is where the rewards are. This is where most human resources management systems provide reinforcement. Summiting is different. It's the long, hard slog, the steep ascent, the lonely road. Summiting is often done in obscurity when no one is watching, the incentives have dried up, and the thrill is gone. It comes down to grinding discipline—when no one is holding you accountable but yourself. Finally, we often mistake momentum for completion because, on appearance, starting looks like finishing. Our heart and mind may be elsewhere. We may just be behaviorally compliant for a little while.

What does it take to summit? It takes a person whose capacity to endure planned deprivation is stronger than his or her desire for instant gratification. That's a fancy way of saying that you'd rather take a bag of marshmallows later rather than one marshmallow now. To summit is to endure for a greater reward. Does that sound like something our popular culture would espouse? That's part of the problem. Our popular culture has nothing but reproach and merry disdain for the values that lead to summiting and nothing but vulgar, narcissistic adoration for the values that lead to starting. Society seems to teach us less and less about summiting. And yet all of the signal accomplishments of humankind are feats of finishing. On second thought, you might want to finish that cheeseburger.

Taking Your Achievement X-Ray

To sustain a long-term pattern of achievement, it's helpful to know the anatomy of your own motivation. The Achievement X-Ray (Figure 6.2) is designed to help you understand how you are personally motivated to achieve based on the external motivators of recognition, rewards, and responsibility. These external motivators don't replace the intrinsic motivation that achieving creates, yet it's important to understand your outside motivators and how they may help you climb the mountains you choose to climb.

To take your Achievement X-Ray, do the following:

Step 1. Review the definition of each of the three external achievement motivators:

> **Recognition:** Public praise, approval, and commendation received as a consequence of achievement
> **Responsibility:** Increased responsibility, accountability, or advancement received as a consequence of achievement
> **Rewards:** Monetary and nonmonetary rewards received as a consequence of achievement

Step 2. Using a 7-to-1 scale, where 7 is high and 1 is low, rate the degree to which you are personally motivated to achieve based on each motivator. For example, ask yourself, "How motivated am I to achieve in order to be recognized?" Put your rating in Figure 6.2 under *Recognition*. Now do the same thing with other two achievement motivators.

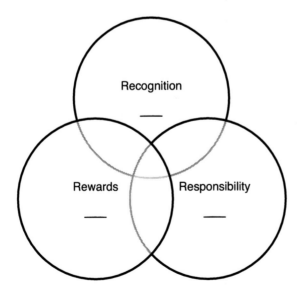

FIGURE 6.2   Your Achievement X-Ray

Step 3. Once you have captured your rating for each of the three achievement motivators, enter it in Table 6.3 and write a brief explanation of why you gave that particular rating. Our hope is that you come to know your external motivational profile better.

Step 4. Finally, with your Achievement X-Ray in hand, identify opportunities you could focus on to add additional fuel to your motivation. Write these opportunities in the last column of Table 6.3. For example, if you're motivated externally by recognition, look for opportunities to get involved in projects, committees, or community events that are highly visible. The acknowledgment, praise, and thanks you'll receive will propel you in your achieving cycle. If you are highly motivated by responsibility, you should sign up for assignments that give you a chance to lead teams or groups of people, projects that will help advance your career or help you learn and grow. If you are

TABLE 6.3   Opportunities to Fuel Your Motivation

Achievement Motivator	External Motivation Score (1 = low; 7 = high)	Explanation	Opportunities
Recognition: Public praise, approval, and commendation received as a consequence of achievement			
Responsibility: Increased responsibility, accountability, or advancement received as a consequence of achievement			
Rewards: Monetary and nonmonetary rewards received as a consequence of achievement			

highly motivated by economic and noneconomic rewards, find your own carrots. Where are they, and how can you get them?

Conclusion

"Happiness does not lie in happiness, but in the achievement of it."

Fyodor Dostoevsky, Russian novelist

Bill Walton had a prominent career in the National Basketball Association. He earned the league's Most Valuable Player award and won two NBA championships. When asked for his take on a college basketball game in which a talented team was beaten by a far less talented team, he said, "The great thing about what they did was they represented all of the things that make life so special. They won the battle of substance over hype, the triumph of achievement over erratic flailing, the conquest of discipline over gambling, the triumph of executing an organized game plan over just hoping that you're going to be lucky, hot, or in the zone. They also represented the conquest of sacrifice, hard work, and commitment to achievement over the pipe dream that someone is going to give you something, or that you can take a pill, or turn a key to get what you want." Then came his final thought: "Never mistake activity for achievement."[10]

Most people are busy, but many people are not achieving. They may be confusing activity with achievement. Yet the achievement cycle is simple. It helps us conclude that for those who aren't achieving the way they want to, achieving is more likely a "want to" problem rather than a "how to" problem.

The good news is that jumping into an achievement cycle is possible at any time. It's a learned behavior that replenishes energy, boosts confidence, increases capacity, and deepens fulfillment.

Tips for Leaders

Teresa M. Amabile and Steven J. Kramer conducted an interesting study that looked at what employees are thinking and feeling as they go about their work, and how leaders can use this information to help job performance. Their research concluded, "The most important managerial behaviors don't involve giving people daily pats on the back or attempting to inject lighthearted fun into the workplace. Rather, they involve two fundamental things: enabling people to move forward in their work, and treating them decently as human beings."[11]

Leaders can have a big impact in helping others achieve by taking those principles to heart. Listed below are tips to help leaders do that very thing and enable their employees to achieve more.

- ☐ **Ask yourself the following questions about how your employees achieve:**

    Do I know the goals my employees are working on in their achieving cycles (personal and professional)?

    What are the roadblocks getting in the way of their progress? What am I doing to remove those roadblocks?

    Is there a clear connection between their professional work and the important work of the team? How can I strengthen that connection and help them understand it clearly?

    Are they overloaded with minutiae or busywork? What can I do to eliminate this type of work?

    Do I know how each employee is motivated? What actions can I take to enhance their motivation?

- ☐ **Set clear goals with employees.** People make more progress when leaders are clear about the link between what they do and what matters to the organization. And successful teams are those that have clear goals, and where people know how their work affects those goals. Help your people gain line-of-sight visibility from their work to the team's goals.

- ☐ **Help employees break projects, goals, and work assignments into small victories.** Small victories tap into motivation. Achieving is fueled by making small amounts of progress, such as accomplishing a task or solving a problem. Help those that work with you jump into an achievement cycle and experience the benefits and rewards of moving through all five steps.

- ☐ **Teach people how to manage time and energy wisely.** Coach employees to fully engage in the task at hand, focus on the important rather than the urgent, avoid distractions, and create balance and renewal in the achievement of the goal. Help them learn to say no to urgent requests or terrific ideas that aren't aligned with the important work of the team.

- ☐ **Commit resources and remove roadblocks.** Enable people to move forward in their work by committing appropriate resources, removing obstacles, helping them work across boundaries, and aligning processes, structure, and systems.

- ☐ **Help employees engage others.** Encourage those you work with to reach out and engage others with similar goals. Remind them that goals can be created independently, but achieving them almost always requires help and support from others.

- ☐ **Identify specific motivators and adjust accordingly.** Discuss with employees their extrinsic motivators, and identify opportunities and implications to bolster the achieving cycle. If they are motivated by recognition, identify ways to give meaningful praise, show approval for their work and team behaviors, or commend them for achievements along the way. Find ways to acknowledge them in front of their peers and express appreciation. If they are motivated by rewards, identify both economic and noneconomic rewards that you can give as a consequence of achievement.

- ☐ **Discuss achieving opportunities outside of work.** Have conversations with employees about what they want to achieve in their careers and in their personal lives. Highly engaged individuals find sources of motivation inside and outside of work. Talk about all aspects of achieving, knowing that the organization still benefits whether an employee becomes more engaged from working with an outside volunteer organization or from working on a project to solve one of your biggest customer complaints. Genuine interest and a little flexibility on your part can go a long way toward increasing motivation, achievement, and ultimately engagement.

☐ **Adjust motivators over time.** Stay connected with your employees. Remember that people's motivations can, and often do, change over time. Have achieving conversations with employees regularly, preferably outside of the annual performance review process. Adjust as they adjust.

7

Contribute: Get Beyond Yourself!

"No man is so poor as to have nothing worth giving:
As well might the mountain streamlets say they have
nothing to give the sea because they are not rivers. Give
what you have."

Henry Wadsworth Longfellow

Your Last Day of Work

Imagine that it's your last day of work. You've been on the job
for 40 years. You've gathered your things and said your good-
byes. You stand up from your desk for the last time and head for
the door. And then it dawns on you that you have to stop by the
human resources department for a short exit interview—that per-
functory ritual that organizations perform, that last opportunity
to glean valuable feedback from the departing employee.

When you walk into the department, the assistant motions you
to a chair in a small conference room. And then, of course, we
walk in to conduct the interview. No surprise there. You're expecting us.

We greet you with a handshake and a smile. You sigh deeply,
sensing perhaps for the first time in your professional life the

complete absence of tension or stress. It's a contemplative moment that deserves a long pause, a moment that will never come again.

We finally start: "It's your last day."

"I know. It's hard to believe. It hasn't quite registered yet."

"It will take some time, I'm sure," one of us offers reassuringly. "Well, we don't want to keep you, so let's get started. As you might expect, we have a standard set of questions that we like to ask in our exit interviews. On second thought, let's skip all that. We just have one question."

"One question?"

"Yep, that's it."

"Okay," you reply, looking a bit surprised.

"Here's the question: What do you value most about the experience you've had here?"

"That's it? That's what you want to know?"

"That's it. Just tell us what matters the most."

You cup your chin in your hand, breathe slowly, and scan the room.

"Well ..."

What would you say if this exit interview were real? Did you know that the response pattern to this question is strikingly consistent? In the past few years, we've asked this question to more than 1,000 employees from all sorts of organizations, industries, and levels of responsibility. More than 90 percent of the time, the top two answers are the same. Can you guess what they are?

Number one: relationships. Number two: personal contribution. Everything else fades away.

When a friend of ours was 18 years old, his father went overseas on a business trip. His father never came home. He was tragically killed by thieves who attempted to rob him in his hotel. At this man's funeral, not a thing was said about his education or accomplishments, not a thing about his money or possessions, not a thing about his titles or travels or triumphs. Instead, his friends and family measured his life by his relationships and his personal contribution to their lives.

> *"When you cease to make a contribution, you begin to die."*
>
> Eleanor Roosevelt

We spoke to our friend just the other day, and he mentioned the symbolic importance of his dad's life. He said his dad's untimely death brought life into sharper relief. Even now, what lingers in his mind is the things said at his dad's funeral—as well as the things that were conspicuously left unsaid. People sifted and sorted through the remains of his legacy. They enshrined as part of his memory the things that mattered most: his relationships and personal contribution. The rest was discarded as fleeting, transitory, and insignificant. Our friend's father remains his hero because he knew the answer to the question of what matters most before his last day came.

It's a curious thing that whether it's your last day of work or your last day of life, the answer to the question of what matters most is the same. How much would it be worth to you to know that before the last day comes? Well, here's the answer—relationships and personal contribution. Thought you'd like to know.

What Is Contribution?

We define contribution as effort directed beyond self. It's a universal driver of engagement. We consider it the ultimate and culminating driver because it brings the other drivers together and gives them higher expression and purpose.

Contributing is effort directed beyond self toward a meaningful purpose.

Think about it for a minute. The other five drivers increase engagement because they bring direct personal rewards.

- If I can shape my work, I'm more engaged.
- If I connect more deeply to the mission of my organization, I'm more engaged.
- If I continue to learn, I'm more engaged.
- If I stretch, I gain more capacity and confidence and I'm more engaged.
- If I achieve something meaningful, I'm more engaged.

All true. All important. But did you notice a pattern? When you apply the other drivers, the benefits go directly to you, and they are what engages you. Contributing is different. When you contribute, the benefits don't go directly to you. They go somewhere else, to something or someone else. Contributing is a fundamentally different driver. It takes you outside of yourself. It's not about you; it's something greater. And by some miracle that we don't fully understand, contributing produces a more powerful kind of engagement.

When you think about contribution as a driver of engagement, think about it on two dimensions. The first one is scope. Are you contributing to others, perhaps a group or the organization? Perhaps even the whole world? Maybe. Or perhaps you're just contributing to a single individual. Does it matter? Isn't a bigger scope of contribution more valuable? Not remotely. Professor Clayton Christensen of the Harvard Business School, the world's foremost expert on innovation, said, "I've concluded that the metric by which God will assess my life isn't dollars but the individual people whose lives I've touched."[1]

"You're the happiest while you're making the greatest contribution."

Robert F. Kennedy

The second dimension is visibility. Is it a public or a private act? Are you going to be recognized for it? Here, too, we can't say that an acknowledged contribution is more important than one that is kept hidden. For example, an employee learned that her colleague had been diagnosed with cancer. Knowing that she would need extra time off to receive her chemo treatments, this individual went to the human resources department and anonymously donated some of her vacation time to her colleague. Was that invisible contribution less valuable than a public act?

From these two dimensions, we're able to identify four main types of contribution, as shown in Figure 7.1. You can contribute publicly or privately. You can also contribute to an individual or more broadly to a group, an organization, or the greater good— what we call a *general* contribution. It's nice to be recognized by your peers. Public contribution is a good thing. But don't underestimate the power of private contribution. Many of the highly engaged people we studied prefer to contribute in quiet ways. They tell us there's nothing sweeter and more fulfilling.

Given these categories, let's consider an example for each one.

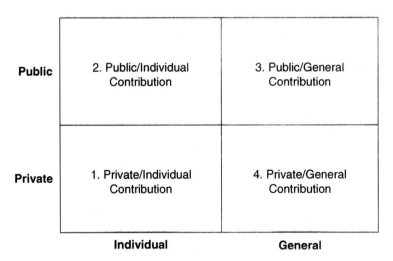

FIGURE 7.1   The Four Types of Contribution

Type 1: Private/Individual Contribution—"The Haystack"

Conrad Gottfredson tells a story: I grew up in a farming town of 700 people, give or take a few. There were more cows than people. My father, Arthur Gottfredson, ran a 200-acre, 50-Holstein dairy farm. He also taught high school math and coached wrestling. Most of his days began at 4 a.m. and ended at 10:30 p.m. He was busy, but always on the lookout for some way to contribute. As a young boy, I was often conscripted to tag along when someone needed help. Dad always made it clear that whatever we did was to be kept quiet. I've since learned that I didn't always tag along. There were occasions when Dad made contributions that I never knew about. When Dad passed away, my mother shared with me an example of a private/individual contribution.

Our neighbor and fellow farmer, Cameron Norton, had finished cutting his hay one year. He had just enough hay to feed his cattle through the winter. On an October afternoon his haystack caught fire and burned to the ground. He was devastated. There was no insurance and no way to replace the hay. How would he feed his cattle for the next six months? Cameron probably didn't sleep that night. Neither did my dad.

My father returned home from his farm work much later than usual the next evening, in fact, just in time to grab a couple hours of sleep prior to the milking turn. He smelled like smoke, so Mom asked him what he'd been doing. "Just working," Dad replied.

The next day, Cameron went out to his hay yard and discovered a fresh stack of hay covering the charred spot where his hay had burned—enough to see him through to the spring. Except for Mom, no one ever knew what Dad had done in the dark of that fall night in Circleville.

> *"We must not, in trying to think about how we can*
> *make a big difference, ignore the small daily differences*

we can make which, over time, add up to the big differ-
ences that we often cannot foresee."

Marian Wright Edelman, U.S. social reformer

Type 2: Public/Individual Contribution— "The Football Coach"

Tim tells a story: As a college football player at Brigham Young University, I had the rare opportunity to be coached by a legend, LaVell Edwards. Coach Edwards has since taken his place in the pantheon of pigskin generals. As a hall-of-famer, he is accorded legend status, a distinction reserved for a small, elite fraternity of coaches who break from the ranks and set themselves apart.

It's one thing to win a championship. It's an entirely different matter to win over and over, to make winning the norm, to cast a culture whose very DNA is engineered to win, to create muscle memory in an institution so that its natural motion propels it to victory.

Most coaches have winning moments. Coach Edwards created a winning era. Let me put this in perspective. In 29 years as head football coach at BYU, Coach Edwards posted only one losing season. Legends build legacies, and then there's everybody else. You get the point.

As a cultural artifact, football is a piece of Americana. It's a game of strategy and toughness. It's a game of performance and accountability. The yardstick by which we measure success in this rarefied world is simple—the win column. If you notch wins, you stay. If you don't, someone moves you on.

We lionize the winners and forget about the losers, but that's just my preamble. What about the rest of the story? Coach Edwards did more than just win football games. Let me tell you about the LaVell Edwards I played for, the LaVell Edwards I observed and studied. As a player, I took mental notes for four years because

I knew that I had been given the opportunity to be a part of something special.

I was learning at the feet of one of the greats, and the lessons being taught extended far beyond the gridiron. Coach Edwards was in the leadership development business. On the ground and in the trenches, he never ceased to teach, and only when necessary did he use words. He contributed to my life in a profoundly personal way and taught me specific lessons that have stuck with me. Here are just three:

Manage Your Emotions for Performance

Coach Edwards was a model of poise under pressure. Regardless of the situation, his outward expression of leadership was calm and confident. Long experience had tutored him to understand that the emotions of fear, anxiety, anger, and frustration are almost always counterproductive in helping an organization achieve its goals. In most cases, the mismanagement of emotions is damaging and increases the risk of failure, especially when people are fatigued and falling behind.

As an organization runs at maximum exertion and draws down its energy reserves, it becomes more vulnerable to discouragement and self-doubt. While everyone is human, the leader must maintain focus in the midst of adversity. Rest assured, there will be adversity and there will be failures. We lost some heartbreakers, but those were the times when Coach Edwards became the repository of our fears and the hope of our renewed efforts.

His focus was on the goal and the development of the players, not on himself. Contrast that with leaders who indulge in negative emotions that lower the productive capacity of their organizations.

Yes, people respond to threats and melodrama in the short term. But over 29 years? I don't think so. Ultimately, high performance is based on a willing offering of discretionary effort. Only a leader's managed, controlled, and checked emotional performance will motivate people to do their best work—and Coach Edwards had an unflappable demeanor. He didn't make use of the customary power tools that we see so much of in the prevailing culture of football. No screaming. No profanity. No head games. No manipulation—just rock-jawed poise.

Seek Unedited Self-Awareness

Some people believe in the distinction between a private reality and a public image. Coach Edwards would laugh at such a notion. He was eminently aware of his amplified public role, but he didn't spend time cultivating a separate persona for public consumption. He simply achieved a high level of self-awareness and then was true to himself in every situation.

Becoming a leader is a process in which the scales of limited self-awareness gradually fall from our eyes, but it doesn't happen by accident. It's a consequence of developing the ability to listen to feedback. It's a willingness to have a truthful encounter with one's own unvarnished truth. Coach Edwards saw himself in the response of others to him. He was exceptionally attuned to his modeling influence and his ability to scale impact. There was humility in his interactions. As a coach he was self-possessed but not arrogant.

You've heard it said that infatuation clouds judgment. I would argue that infatuation with oneself clouds judgment even more. Some coaches become single-member mutual admiration societies. That's when it gets dangerous.

Coach Edwards maintained his self-awareness through modesty and self-restraint. He was keenly aware that everyone was watching his every move. Because there was no distinction between the private citizen and the public figure, he wasn't confused, and neither were his players.

Care About Players More than the Game

I learned from Coach Edwards that notions of professional distance and stuffy paternalism are silly concepts that engage and inspire no one. In disposition, Coach Edwards was disarming, pleasant, friendly, and self-effacing. He was genuinely interested in his players, not just the X's and O's.

After practice, we'd be at the training table (cafeteria) eating dinner as a team, and Coach Edwards would be doing his trademark ritual, making the rounds with a bowl of tapioca pudding in his hands.

On Sunday mornings, when we were banged up and sitting in ice baths, he would do his rounds again to inspect the wounded and give a word of encouragement. Why? Because we needed it.

You see, football is a reflection of life. It's just a more transparent plane. If you play Division I football, your chance of injury is 100 percent. The only question is severity. But that's not unlike any other field of endeavor. We all take some pretty rough shots, and it doesn't hurt to have a leader around who cares when you get the soup knocked out of you.

Some leaders obsess on a need to be large and in charge. What a tragedy to live on the dark side of charisma. What a shame to repel people with a false sense of openness. Coach Edwards made it abundantly clear that it's impossible to build an organization and summon its institutional will if you don't really like people. You may get lucky and win a championship, but you'll end up leaving a landfill, not a legacy.

During his career, Coach Edwards earned a room full of trophies and a bag full of garish championship rings—the customary emblems of the win column. More than that, he earned the admiration, respect, and loyalty of a generation of broken-down football players who stand when he enters the room. John Quincy Adams observed, "If your actions inspire others to dream more, learn more, do more, and become more, you are a leader." My old coach—that stone-faced visage, that genuine article, that iconic builder of men—contributed to many lives, and in a very personal way, he contributed to mine.

Type 3: Public/General Contribution—
"A Dent in the Universe"

The only thing conformist about Steve Jobs was his black turtle-neck. Nearly everything else about him was bold and distinctive. What we admire most about him was his capacity for independent thought and action. When it comes right down to it, it's a characteristic that's not as prevalent in humans as you would think, or at least it lies dormant in most of us. Steve Jobs had it in abundance from the beginning. "Don't be trapped by dogma," he said. "Don't let the noise of others' opinions drown out your own inner voice." Strong personalities have this quality of independence. The question is what to do with it, how to give it expression. Steve Jobs was bound to influence a lot and be influenced a little. He was born an independent variable—a cause rather than an effect.

He deserves our admiration and study for his unique contribution. His life was many things. He had galactic vision. He was a great technologist. He was a genius of design, a charismatic showman, and a peerless marketer. He cultivated a discerning eye for consumer preference and taste. He was also hard to work with, a tyrant at times, and quite egotistical.

What's not in question is that he made a contribution—quite a spectacular contribution. He became one of the greatest innovators in history. It looked as if the story was over when he left Apple in 1985, cast out from the company he had cofounded. Yet he was to return 11 years later "a very different person," as he would later say. But it was more than an unlikely comeback. His trajectory from that point was beyond imagination. In his second act, he would launch the iMac, the iPod, iTunes, the iPhone, and the iPad. He would literally change the world.

When Jobs was young, he was an enfant terrible—a loner, disruptive and curious. After high school, he went to college for six months and then dropped out. He became a smelly hippie and, by his own admission, had no idea what he wanted to do with his life. But he loved technology, so he wandered back home, and you know the rest of the story. He and his partner Steve Wozniak started Apple in Jobs's parents' garage. It was here that Jobs's unencumbered personality would find meaningful expression. Out of his disdain for convention, out of his prickly, brash, narcissistic temperament, out of his vision, high drive, and confidence, out of his aesthetic instincts and a deep emotional need to create something of elegant form and hyperfunction came an unprecedented string of exquisitely designed products and platforms.

Jobs had made heroic mistakes in the past. He had crashed and burned. But out of his failures he fine-tuned his judgment, refined his taste, and elevated his unreasonable expectations. He developed an empathy for and connection to the consumer that was astonishing. "A lot of times," he said, "people don't know what they want until you show it to them." He proved true his theory that "simple can be harder than complex." Our Apple devices are simple —and absolutely elegant.

Steve Jobs did not practice conventional corporate leadership. He was its implacable foe. Most organizations in the world foster incremental growth through incremental improvement. Most corporate leaders compete as a direct response to their competitors. They benchmark the herd. They look for best practices, and in the context of that arena, figure out what to do next. They lead in response to the measures and countermeasures of others. How much time do you think Steve Jobs spent looking for best practices among his competitors?

Did he come up with all of the ideas? Of course not. And that's part of the point. He cultivated a culture of independent thought and action because he had the seeds to plant it. We can only hope the seeds he planted will grow a few more of the disruptive and curious variety—the kind that change the world.

Here's the question: Did contributing drive Jobs's level of engagement? Need we ask? He put it this way: "And a lot of us want to contribute something back to our species and to add something to the flow. It's about trying to express something in the only way that most of us know how—because we can't write Bob Dylan songs or Tom Stoppard plays. We try to use the talents we do have to express our deep feelings, to show our appreciation to all the contributions that came before us, and to add something to that flow. That's what has driven me."[2]

Type 4: Private/General Contribution—"The Physician"

Consider the life of an 87-year-old physician, Dr. Doug Heiner, who went from coal mining roots to teaching medicine at Harvard, and then on to become chief of Pediatric Immunology and Allergy at Harbor-UCLA Medical Center. Dr. Heiner maintains that his greatest professional contribution was a very simple thing he did during the Korean War back in 1951. As a medic, he was given responsibility for preventive medicine for all Korean military medical units. In his spare time, he decided to lend a hand at a two-tent civilian hospital in Pocheon, South Korea. He befriended two Korean doctors there and focused his energies on children because he had already been accepted for specialist training in pediatrics at Harvard University.

After the Korean conflict ended, Doug returned home and carried on with his advanced training. But he didn't forget the two doctors he had worked with at the two-tent hospital in Pocheon. He used his influence to help Dr. E. Hyock Kwon and Dr. Ko Kwang Wook receive additional training in the United States. Dr. Kwon earned a doctorate in public health. After returning to Korea, he became chairman of the Department of Public Health at Seoul National University's College of Medicine, the largest and most prestigious medical school in the country. Later, he became dean of the College of Medicine. His rise in influence continued, and he became president of Seoul National University, Minister of Education for the Republic of Korea, Minister of Health and Social Affairs, and later Minister of the Environment. He also served a term as president of the Republic of Korea National Academy of Sciences.

The other physician, Dr. Ko, decided to specialize in pediatrics and received two years of pediatric residency in Seoul. Doug recommended Dr. Ko for further training at Harvard, which provided him more advanced training in pediatrics than anyone in Korea had at the time. He ultimately became head of the Pediatric Department at Seoul National University while Dr. Kwon was dean of the college. Later, these two physicians established a new children's hospital at Seoul National University. Professor Ko became the first medical director and helped the institution become one of the finest children's hospitals in Asia.

On one of Doug's visits to Korea, Dr. Ko took him on a tour of the new children's hospital. When he finished the tour, Dr. Ko looked at Dr. Heiner and said, "You made all of this possible." Later, Doug would write, "When I reflect on the simple decision I made to stop in for repeated, brief visits with Drs. Kwon and Ko in their two-tent Pocheon hospital, I consider it one of the most important decisions I have made in my life. If I hadn't, Dr. Ko may not have decided to become a pediatrician. He certainly would not have had the opportunity to train in the Children's Medical Center in Boston. It is thrilling to me to observe that two doctors, when afforded the opportunities needed to develop their talents, could accomplish such astonishing things. I consider this one of the greatest things I have been privileged to do."[3]

Dr. Heiner's simple gesture to befriend two struggling physicians in the midst of war became much more than a personal contribution to two lives. It multiplied and became a larger contribution to thousands of children and even the nation itself.

This brings us to another observation about contribution: it can be assigned or unassigned. Both are rewarding. Both elevate engagement. The question is whether you contribute in unassigned ways, as the woman who donated her vacation days to her cancer-afflicted friend did. Once again, the highly engaged report that in many ways it's the unassigned forms of contribution that drive engagement the most.

How important is contribution? Let's put it this way: If the other drivers of engagement don't translate into contribution, they lose their value and impact. If you only shape for your own benefit, connect for your own benefit, learn for your own benefit, stretch for your own benefit, and achieve for your own benefit, your life becomes small, boring, and pretty stale. As a matter of fact, if you live and work unto yourself, life starts to lose its meaning.

A line in a poem from Marianne Williamson says, "Your playing small does not serve the world." The poem encourages us to contribute, but does it suggest that small contributions are not valuable? Does it suggest that you need a big title and a big position to make a real contribution? Certainly not. The key message is that we need to get outside of ourselves, regardless of our sphere of influence.

There need not be a conflict between personal gain, contribution in the workplace, and benefit to society. The three can go hand in hand. When an employee feels supported and empowered in achieving her goals, her engagement and contribution increase. But how many of us work for enlightened organizations? Perhaps we don't view our organization as enlightened, but there's a way to take charge of our contribution even if we do it alone.

> *"You are not here merely to make a living. You are here to enable the world to live more amply, with greater vision, and with a finer spirit of hope and achievement. You are here to enrich the world. You impoverish yourself if you forget this errand."*
>
> Woodrow Wilson, President of the United States
> (1913–1921)

Level 1 Contribution: *What* You Do

Let's suppose that all of the tasks you're responsible for in your current job are like a basket of eggs. It's your job to deliver the eggs. But they're not all the same. You have white eggs, brown eggs, and blue eggs. The white eggs are the basic tasks, the brown eggs are the building tasks, and the blue eggs are the bonus tasks.

- White eggs: basic tasks
- Brown eggs: building tasks
- Blue eggs: bonus tasks

White Eggs or Basic Tasks

You long for the day you don't have to deliver a single white egg. But you know that's wishful thinking. That day will never come. We all have basic tasks we have to complete. We certainly don't relish these tasks, but it's stuff that has to get done and someone's got to do it. For the teacher, it might be the budget planning meeting. For the nurse, it might be filling out endless reports to meet regulatory requirements. For the salesperson, it might be providing forecasts, updating the sales pipeline, and detailing the most recent sales opportunities. For the reporter, it's attending yet another boring press conference. You get the picture.

It's most often the administrative tasks that we dislike the most. But they have to get done. We all have white eggs that need to be delivered, and we can't delegate the task to someone else. We're the end of the line. Delivering our white eggs is usually a condition of employment. We have to do it, so we may as well do it well. Yet delivering white eggs is seldom a big driver of engagement. We don't enjoy it. Our natural inclination is to spend as little time as possible delivering white eggs so we can move on to more exciting work.

Brown Eggs or Building Tasks

Delivering brown eggs is a lot more fun because brown eggs are harder to deliver. We have to draw on our knowledge, experiences, and skills. Delivering brown eggs over the course of a career requires that we keep investing in our ongoing personal development.

For the teacher, delivering brown eggs means preparing and teaching the students. For the doctor, it means diagnosing and treating the patient. For the sales professional, it means finding a solution that meets a customer's need. For the reporter, it means investigating and reporting the story. Delivering brown eggs creates more value for the organization and more reward for us personally because building tasks are usually more fun and more challenging than many of the mundane maintenance tasks we have to complete. In other words, cooking dinner is more rewarding than washing the dishes after dinner.

Blue Eggs or Bonus Tasks

Delivering blue eggs is the final and most rewarding task—what we call a bonus task. To deliver a blue egg is to make a unique and distinctive contribution. For a teacher, it might be having the ability to motivate and influence a particular student who is struggling. For a doctor, it might mean sitting on a panel to develop a new treatment. For a sales professional, it could be the chance to develop a new global account. For a reporter, it might be breaking a story on a hidden issue. Delivering a blue egg is perhaps the most motivating part of professional life.

Steve's Blue Egg

Alistair Aitchison tells a story: My friend Steve is a civil engineer working for a UK-based utilities company. For many years he has consistently delivered quality white and brown eggs—the basic and building tasks that make up his role. His reputation within the organization is excellent, and through his personal credibility, he has been able to approach his line manager to gain support for a blue egg idea.

Steve encountered a charity organization called Water Aid and found that its work included the need for volunteer civil engineers to assist in the development of water supplies for villages in Africa. He investigated the opportunity and requested that his organization sponsor his participation by supporting him in joining the Water Aid team for a week. Taking his request up the management chain, his line manager discovered that the company had a social responsibility policy that encourages such participation. He also realized that working with Water Aid would be good press for the organization and could help recruit top graduates from universities and new hires from other organizations.

As a result of his participation in this charity work (delivering this blue egg), Steve was able to meet his personal objective of making a difference in a way that made use of his skills and experience. At the same time, Steve has gained a cultural experience that has become highly motivating and valuable to him. While participating in this charity work, Steve has come into contact with engineers from other organizations in other parts of the world. By participating, Steve has gained new skills that he has applied to other aspects of his work.

Here's our most interesting discovery about job roles. Every job includes a basket of white and brown eggs that need to be delivered. In fact, if you look at almost any documented job description, it lists a series of basic and building tasks—white and brown eggs. What's conspicuously absent is the blue eggs. Rarely will you encounter a job description that lists any blue eggs or bonus tasks. Why? Because delivering blue eggs is not a normal expectation of the organization. That's why we call them bonus tasks. They're beyond the call of duty. Job descriptions are written for the average employee doing a job in an average, albeit acceptable, way.

What's the consequence of an average employee doing an average job in an average way? Average engagement, of course! We soon discover that blue eggs are a matter of personal discretion and motivation. The organization will rarely ask you to deliver a blue egg—to find a new or distinctive way to add value. It's up to you to find the blue egg and then deliver it.

To contribute to the organization and build a highly satisfying career along the way, you have to manage all your eggs. Regardless of your talent, you can't deliver only blue eggs. That doesn't work either. You have to manage the mix.

Master the Basics

Contribution is built from the ground up. It begins with your ability to perform the basic tasks that are assigned to your role, your white eggs. Before you spend a minute entertaining thoughts of contributing in some big way, stop right there. Have you mastered the essential tasks of your job? There's really nothing to talk about until you do. You simply can't pass "Go" until you master the basics. This is how you build credibility. As you do, you will be given the opportunity to do more and to contribute in different ways.

Highly engaged employees share this pattern. They start with the basics. They learn to deliver white eggs with accuracy and speed. Then they learn to deliver brown eggs with quality and consistency. At that point, and only at that point, do they look for opportunities to deliver blue eggs, to pursue bonus tasks that engage their special interests and make use of their special gifts.

You may be saying to yourself, "That's just lovely, but I'm up to my waist in white and brown eggs. I can't even deliver all of them right now. There's simply no time to even think about blue eggs."

We promise you that we know the feeling. We've been there. Suspend your disbelief for just a minute. Let's see if there just might be an opportunity to manage the delivery of white and brown eggs a little better.

Your Egg Basket

Using the worksheet in Table 7.1, take a few minutes to list the tasks that consume your time in a typical week. For each task, estimate the percentage of time required to complete it. List all major tasks or categories of tasks until you allocate 100 percent of your time.

Next, indicate what egg color the task represents. Basic tasks are white. Building tasks are brown. Bonus tasks are blue.

Examine the way you spend your time overall. Would you like to shift the way you allocate your time? In the final right-hand column, indicate the way you would like to spend your time among your various tasks. It may not be possible to do everything you want, but if you could shift a little bit, how would you do it?

Consider using this table as a tool for a development discussion with your line manager. At a minimum, check the time you're spending on your assigned tasks against the importance of each task. In other words, ask yourself if it all makes sense.

TABLE 7.1   Egg Basket Worksheet

Tasks	Type	Time Now	Time in the Future
List all of the tasks that are a part of your role.	What type of task is it? Is it a white, brown, or blue egg?	What percentage of time in a week do you spend completing this task now?	What percentage of time in a week would you like to spend on this task in the future?

Level 2 Contribution: *How* You Do It

So far we've addressed what you do by focusing on your egg basket. But there's another way to look at things: *how* you do them. In the 1980s, the United Kingdom saw the emergence of a new era of musicians. Among them was one of the first girl bands, Bananarama. Collaborating with another band from that era, Fun Boy Three, they produced a remake of a jazz song first recorded in 1939 by Jimmie Lunceford, Harry James, and Ella Fitzgerald called "T'ain't What You Do. It's the Way That You Do It." If you haven't heard the song, look it up and have a listen. It's a catchy tune, and it captures the point of level 2 contribution. In addition to the "what," it's the "how" that counts. How we approach our work has a huge impact on our contribution and level of engagement. There are five main ways that a person contributes within an organization (see Figure 7.2). You can contribute as a private, learner, expert, coach, or visionary.

If you continue to develop professionally, you will advance from one role to the next as a natural progression. If you stop developing, you won't. Let's take a closer look at each one. As we do, follow along and ask yourself if you fit one of the profiles more than the others.

The Private

The term *private* comes from the military. It denotes a soldier of the lowest rank. We're not suggesting that we're all soldiers, but the term captures the essence of what's required in the first stage of contributing. To be a private is to learn to manage yourself for

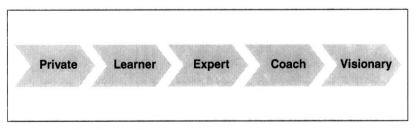

FIGURE 7.2 **Five Ways to Contribute**

performance. You begin by applying basic discipline in your own life. There are two essential performance requirements for the beginner: First, show up. Second, follow through.

Key Private Behaviors

- Showing up
- Following through

Organizations naturally expect all employees to do these two things. They represent the basis of all performance. If you can, you transition immediately to becoming a learner. If you can't, you will struggle to learn because learning includes showing up and following through.

You may be a bit surprised that we mention such basic requirements. It's unfortunate, but there are still many people who begin working in an organization and yet never have learned these two basic requirements of performance. In fact, we estimate that if you simply show up and follow through, you may actually outperform half of the working population. Our popular culture simply isn't teaching people to be reliable and ethical in what they commit to do. When you learn to show up and follow through, you have become brilliant on the basics and are ready to move to the next stage of development.

The Learner

When you first enter the workplace, you're given a number of white and brown eggs to deliver. But the organization understands that you're just starting out. You may not know how to deliver all of the eggs, so you learn as you go. Gradually, you increase your ability to complete the basic and building tasks that are part of your role. As you do, you get help along the way. You'll need guidance from your boss and your colleagues. All of this is part of the normal expectation. It's an intense learning period. The organization is investing in you for the future, hoping that you'll be able to increase your ability to contribute as time goes by.

As a learner, there are key behaviors that will determine your success. Most important, you have to be willing to learn. This means you have to be willing to observe, ask for and receive feedback, and practice delivering white and brown eggs until you can do it on your own. You have to depend on others for advice and guidance, so you have to be coachable. Yes, you'll make mistakes along the way, but you keep trying. The "how" of being a learner is what matters. It's your attitude, your effort, and your reliability that will make the difference. People don't expect you to be an expert. They simply expect you to give your best effort and improve along the way. They expect initiative and follow-through. They expect you to ask questions when you don't understand how to do something.

Now, a question: if we come back five years later and you're still in the learning mode, if you're a junior baker at a bakery and you still can't make bread without help, is that all right? Of course not. There's a natural expectation for you to master the basics of bread making. So it is with the learner. Yes, we're always learning. It's one of the six drivers, but if we don't achieve mastery on basic tasks after an appropriate period of time, we're not making the expected contribution. If you're a helper too long, you'll wake up one day and realize that you've turned into a low performer. That's discouraging. What happens to your level of engagement? That's right: it goes south.

Key Learner Behaviors

- Active learning
- Effective questioning
- Willingness to ask for and receive feedback
- Willingness to cooperate and work with others
- Dependable follow-through
- Ethical conduct

The Expert

The learner never stops learning, but after a while the learner becomes an expert in some things. It goes back to the medieval guild. You began as an apprentice. But that was not a destination. It was a way station on the road to becoming a journeyman, and then eventually a master craftsman or artisan. In the expert stage, you deepen and expand your skills. You take the training wheels off and learn to perform even more complex tasks independently. You begin to build the foundation of your professional identity and personal reputation.

> *"An expert is a man who has made all the mistakes which can be made in a very narrow field."*
>
> Niels Bohr

Staying with our bread-making example, not only can you bake superb bread, but you've expanded your repertoire. Now you can bake the artisan breads—the malted granary, the English country cob, the New York rye, and the Stilton with pear and port chutney. When that gorgeous loaf of roast potato bread comes out of the oven, the aroma wafts its way through the bakery. As your customers light up, your confidence and engagement go to even higher levels. You are now doing your work with a sense of pride and ownership that you have never experienced before. You have a reputation for excellence and quality and a personal brand that reflects that.

Key Expert Behaviors

- Independent performance
- Demonstrated technical expertise
- Collaborative team member
- Multitasking ability
- Delivery of high-quality results

And how does the organization react? The organization is just as pleased as you are. You could continue to contribute this way for years, and both you and the organization would probably be happy. But there's an opportunity to do more. There's an opportunity to "leaven" your contribution, to expand it even more.

The Coach

One day a student of quality guru Dr. W. Edwards Deming asked him what it would take to get an A grade in his class. Another student asked what it would take to get an A+. This is what he said: "An A contribution is when you successfully complete your agreed upon tasks and activities. An A+ contribution is when you help others achieve success in completing their agreed upon tasks and activities."

If you've become an expert in the basic and building tasks of your job, there will surely come a time when you have the opportunity to contribute in a different way. When you become an artisan baker, it's only a matter of time until people want to know what you know and do what you do. It's your choice. When this time comes, you can either shift the way you contribute and coach others or stick to a pattern of working in a more independent and isolated way. You can remain a specialist. But we suggest the former.

Once you become an expert, you naturally have the chance to become a coach. To coach is to train, mentor, guide, and develop others, both formally and informally. It means making your contribution through others, not exclusively, but in a major way that you didn't before. You might think it's natural to impart what you know to others. That's somewhat true. But it's a different thing when you become very deliberate about it, when you actually set goals to develop specific individuals and set aside time to invest in their development. When that becomes a personal priority, when it becomes part of your core stewardship, it requires a different approach. You can't keep doing things the way you were doing them. You have to shift your focus, divert your time and resources, and measure your success in a different way—in the results of others.

When you become a coach, you become a force multiplier. You scale your influence and magnify your impact. The rewards are different too. You feel a rich and deeply satisfying kind of engagement that comes in no other way. Becoming a coach requires an unselfish view toward the development of others. It means wanting to listen and understand another's perspective. Once you become a coach, you can stay a coach for the rest of your life.

> *"It is one of the most beautiful compensations in life that no man can sincerely try to help another without helping himself."*
>
> Ralph Waldo Emerson

But first you have to ask yourself if you want to be a coach. As an expert, you're not necessarily the repository of all the answers. You'll be learning for the rest of your life, but at least you know enough to help others develop. That's the point, and the opportunity that will come your way. For many people, once they start becoming a coach, they start to define success differently. It shifts from a "me" focus to a "you" focus. Coaches say, "Your success is the measure of my success."

The Invisible Law of Compensation

Mike Baer tells a story: years ago, as a young, green pea sales associate, I asked my boss a simple question, "Who is your top performing sales associate, and what does that person do to succeed?" Instead of telling me the answer, he gave me the name of the top producer in the company. His name was Norm, and my boss simply told me to go talk to him. I very timidly approached Norm one day and introduced myself. I told him I was new and needed some help to get started on the right foot. I asked him if he could give me a little advice.

To my utter amazement, Norm took me under his wing. His workload was already heavy and his sales pipeline was bursting at the seams, and yet he made time for me. He came in early and stayed late to help me succeed. He showed me the ropes. Norm taught me that if I learned the skills and disciplines he taught me, I couldn't help but succeed. Actually, it wasn't quite that simple. The reality was that during our time together, I gained confidence under his direction. In fact, my confidence accelerated.

Norm had been with the organization for 17 years when I approached him as a new sales associate. Now I look back and reflect on Norm and the contribution he made to my career and my life. But it didn't end there. Norm had mentored dozens of other sales executives at the company before I got there. In fact, through his influence he saved the careers of several people. He may have saved mine.

One day, after several months of mentoring by Norm, I earned the top sales award at our company for the month. There was no one more proud of me than Norm. He was my biggest fan and cheerleader. I offered to share the gift that came along with the award. Norm would have none of that. He told me his reward was seeing me succeed. He had only one request: find a struggling sales associate, take that person under your wing, and help him or her succeed.

Norm puzzled me. Why would a busy sales executive make time for me? Why would he care about my success? I spoke with him about this in detail the night I won the sales award. To him it was really pretty simple: helping others win helps the organization win, and it always comes back to you. He told me he didn't know how it all worked, but there was some invisible law of compensation that rewards you. He felt more job satisfaction and a much deeper and richer sense of engagement.

If you look around, you'll discover that not everyone is a coach. Not everyone wants to be a coach. Why is that? Our conclusion is quite simple: most people who don't want to contribute through coaching are suffering from either an abundance of ego or a famine of confidence. Otherwise, what would hold you back?

Key Coaching Behaviors

- Openness and accessibility
- Leading through influence rather than authority
- Leading through questioning
- Generosity with time to mentor and help others
- Willingness to be interrupted
- Motivation of others

The Visionary

Global healthcare devices company KCI had as its main focus orthopedic beds. Or it did until one of its sales executives, while visiting a client, observed a healing solution that applied a film and vacuum technology to an incision to accelerate healing from the inside out rather than using a traditional bandage. When this sales executive shared what he had seen with a senior executive within the organization, KCI ended up purchasing the technology, and now the solution accounts for more than 50 percent of the company's annual revenues in a market that's growing at a much higher rate than in the past.

> *"A visionary is one who sees more than others see, who sees farther than others see, and who sees before others see."*
>
> Leroy Eims, author

That's just one example of seeing an opportunity and capitalizing on it. But that's not the point. The point is that he was looking. Unless you're looking for opportunities because you're trying to build the future, you don't see them. Becoming a visionary is no different from becoming a learner, an expert, or a coach. It's a choice to expand the way you contribute. We're not saying you need to be a senior leader or an expert in strategy. And we're not saying that you need to be a natural innovator or a creative genius. At a basic level, to become a visionary is simply to keep your eyes open, look around, and find opportunities and solutions.

If standing still is personal and organizational suicide, it makes all the sense in the world to become a visionary in your own small way. Please don't think that becoming a visionary is the exclusive preserve of executives. That's simply not the case. Almost any executive will tell you that he or she needs more people who can help him or her solve problems and create the future. Think of your company's vision as a mosaic. A mosaic is created by arranging small, colored pieces of tile. As a whole, it may depict a grand scene. But if you stand close, you see the individual pieces that make it up. To contribute even one piece of tile to the mosaic is to be a visionary. You are contributing to the portrait of the future.

How? It comes down to simple things. It starts with the realization that success is never final. It comes from knowing that continuous improvement is a way of life, that the environment is in a constant state of change. Most important, it comes from valuing other human beings, caring about their success, and wanting to make a difference. There's something uniquely satisfying about contributing to the progress and direction of an organization, even if it's something simple.

Key Visionary Behaviors

- Seeing the whole
- Scanning the environment, monitoring and anticipating trends
- Creating a network inside and outside the organization
- Looking for performance gaps and opportunities
- Being curious
- Bringing people together to solve problems
- Challenging assumptions and ways of doing things
- Prioritizing and saying no to good ideas when you can't do everything.

The Relationship Between Behaviors, and Contribution

The relationship between our behaviors and our contribution is clear: behaviors drive contribution, and the type of behaviors drives the type of contribution. Here's the bottom line: as we progress from private to learner, from learner to expert, from expert to coach, and from coach to visionary, we spend more of our time behaving in ways that increase our contribution. Our contribution expands, and so does our value to the organization. Finally, our level of engagement shadows our contribution. The higher our contribution, the higher the level of engagement.

People leave their jobs for a variety of reasons. Chances are that if you leave your job, you're not making the kind of contribution you want to make and the kind you're capable of making. Years of research data tell us that 80 percent of employees don't think they're using their strengths on a daily basis.[4] People tend to disengage slowly and then just leave. We suggest you do just the opposite. Give your organization, your boss, and your job your very best effort. If you're disengaged, reengage slowly on your own initiative by increasing your contribution. Too many employees quit early and unnecessarily because the organization and the job aren't meeting their expectations. In fact, that's the number one reason people leave their jobs. They conclude that "the job or workplace was not as expected."[5] In that situation, most people disengage and then leave. But have you considered the other possibility—to engage and stay?

The challenge for many of us is that our bosses often don't understand the anatomy of contribution. They don't understand the progression of roles and how enlarging your contribution increases engagement. As a result, we end up being pigeonholed into jobs that don't stretch us, don't give us opportunities for growth, fail to provide opportunities to move beyond our current behaviors, and, as a result, trap a lot of our potential without an outlet. Is it any wonder that so many people feel frustrated in the workplace and end up channeling their energies elsewhere?

This untapped contribution that is so often trapped within us is what we call our *discretionary contribution*. It's the equivalent to a seam of gold hidden in a mine. An enlightened organization might recognize the seam and pull it out by empowering and supporting you to take responsibility for your own development while offering support. What if you don't work for one of those enlightened organizations? Again, consider the possibility that you can expand your contribution and engagement on your own. How? Asking yourself these questions might be helpful:

- What are the skills and behaviors that are critical to success in my role?
- Do I demonstrate a high level of competence in those skills and behaviors?
- Compared to others performing a similar role within my organization, am I successful?
- What about compared to others performing a similar role within my industry?
- Do I keep up-to-date with the latest developments and thinking in my area of expertise?
- Is there someone inside or outside of my organization who could help me develop and improve my capabilities so that I can be the best that I can be?

The answers to these questions may help show you where the opportunities to increase your contribution lie.

Earning the Right to Contribute

We were recently working on a project with a team of computer programmers from a software company. There were about eight programmers on this particular team, which was charged with the task of building a new software program.

We sat in several meetings with this team early on in the project. The programmers seemed to respect each other and get along quite well, except for one thing. A consistent pattern of behavior emerged. When one of the programmers offered a suggestion or an idea about how to do something, the other programmers politely ignored him. The more they ignored his ideas, the more ideas he would try to contribute. And the more he would try to contribute, the more they would ignore him. It was painful to watch.

After the meeting, we asked one of the other programmers in private what was going on. The answer was very simple. The programmer who was being ignored was brand new. He had been on the job all of two weeks. The reason he was being ignored was because he had not earned the right to contribute.

One of the things that most organizations do informally is to set up permission rights, and the right to contribute is one of those permission rights that must be earned. The programmer was quite naive and inexperienced, and it really would have made sense for him to be a little more aware of himself and the context. His colleagues were trying to be polite in the way they ignored him, but basically they were saying, "We're happy that you're here, and maybe you'll become the CEO someday, but for now it might be a good idea to listen and learn! Once you get that down, once you establish your professional credibility, then you will be able to put something on the table and we'll take a serious look at it."

Level 3 Contribution: A Long-Term Perspective

Having considered what and how we contribute, let's shift our focus to the long term. Let's think about contribution across a career.

You will go through some transitions in your career. Every time you do, there will be hurdles to overcome. Moving from one role to another requires that we learn new skills and develop new relationships. We have to go back to being a learner, at least for a little while. Similarly, if we change organizations, there will most likely be a new set of processes and procedures that need to be learned and a new culture to adjust to. Finally, if we change industries, there is a whole new world to get used to.

The bigger the change, the more time you'll spend back in the learner phase. What's important to recognize is that transitions take time. The more we are willing to seek help, the quicker and smoother the transition. When we don't get help or clarify expectations, we get frustrated, stretch out the transition period, and increase the chance of failure.

We may not have full control over our formal progression, but we do control whether we make a difference. We can seek out roles and assignments that will make a difference to the organization. When was the last time you volunteered for an assignment? Most important is that we align our contribution with the expectations and priorities of the organization.

The Little Things Are the Big Things

While managing our contribution within the workplace is important, it is our contribution outside of the workplace—within our families, neighborhoods, communities, and even countries—that will ultimately make the most significant difference in our lives and the lives of those around us.

Alistair Aitchison tells a story: my dad taught me two very important things in life—how to golf and how to contribute. On the day of his funeral, my sister Carol and I led a procession that wound its way along the streets of the small Scottish fishing town of Eyemouth, carrying our father's body to be laid to rest in the local graveyard. He had lived his entire life in this small community, touching people's lives with a cheerful and engaging personality and many talents. He even won the local golf-club championship on 11 occasions.

The streets were lined with friends and associates who joined the funeral cortege that made its way to the graveside. As we gathered at his final resting place, I realized that he couldn't even take his golf clubs with him. Golfing had come to an end, but his contribution had not. Here were gathered his friends, the members of this community who came to show their appreciation for his contribution to their lives. I learned another lesson about contribution that day: we don't get to measure our own. Other people do. They get the last word. They measure it for us.

The experience on that bittersweet day taught me a priceless lesson about life: we need to focus our contribution on the things that matter most—the people whose lives we have the opportunity to touch. Most of the time, our contribution consists of small and often seemingly insignificant things. Small acts of assistance, encouragement, guidance, and kindness are the birdies we make on the fairway of life. In the end, these small things constitute the supreme form of contribution.

> *"Do something for somebody every day for which you do not get paid."*
>
> Albert Schweitzer, humanitarian

We touch the lives of others within the workplace, within our families, within our circle of friends, and within our community, and it's the time that we take to listen, understand, and help in some small and yet meaningful way that makes the biggest difference.

To better understand the impact that this contribution can have on our lives, consider this exercise.

Step 1. Identify one person who has made a contribution to your life (professionally or personally) and answer the questions in Table 7.2. Having reflected on what someone did for you and the impact it had on your life, consider how you can do the same for someone else.

Step 2. Identify a person to whom you would like to make a contribution. Identify something that you can do to help

TABLE 7.2   What Someone Has Done for You

What did that person do?

Why do you think that person did it?

Why did what he or she did make a
difference to you?

What did you learn?

TABLE 7.3   What You Could Do for Someone Else

Whom would you like to make a
contribution for?

What needs does he or she have?

What will you do to help this person?

When will you do it?

personally and/or professionally and answer the questions
in Table 7.3. You may want to look for something small.
Don't feel that what you do has to be a big or visible thing.

Perhaps you've seen the movie *Pay It Forward*, starring Helen
Hunt and Kevin Spacey. The expression "pay it forward" means
helping someone else instead of reciprocating to the person that
helped you. Often in life, we don't have the opportunity to repay
the people who contribute to our lives. They move on, and so do
we, and it becomes our chance to find another person to help.

Conclusion

As you reflect on the individuals that had an impact on your early
life—your parents, grandparents, aunts and uncles, brothers and
sisters, brothers- and sisters-in-law, friends, teachers, coaches,
church and youth leaders, and members of your local community—
recognize the sacrifice and contribution they made. Recognize
what they taught you. You'll often find they believed in you more

than you believed in yourself. At some point, we need to cross over and become net contributors rather than net consumers. When you do, your engagement will go to a new level. If you keep it up, you'll rub off on others, and the legacy of your contribution will never end.

Your contribution is indeed under your control. We make choices that determine our success and our happiness in both our personal and professional lives. At regular intervals, take the time in your career and throughout your life to take a step back, reflect, and ask yourself if you're satisfied with your contribution. If you're highly engaged, you're probably making a significant contribution. If you're not, take a second look.

Tips for Leaders

The ability to contribute is within the grasp of every person. And hopefully in this chapter, you've learned why. Contribution is not about feats of daring. It's not about being a hero. It's not about doing things that require extraordinary skill or talent. Contribution is about pointing your effort outside. It's about living outside yourself and contributing to some meaningful purpose or worthy cause. There are plenty out there. You choose.

Once you pick a place to devote some of your time, attention, and energy, get started. It's not hard, and it's not complicated. Even if it's not pretty, any exertion you make to contribute matters.

So if you haven't guessed, the first tip for you as a leader to help others drive engagement through contributing is to contribute yourself. If you're not doing it, don't expect others to. Especially on this driver, you have to lead by example.

To help your employees learn to contribute even faster, here are a few key suggestions for questions and statements you can use to help your employees learn task management in action.

□ **Get clear.** Do you understand the requirements, results, and measures of your job?

□ **Check in.** Seek feedback from your boss and peers on a frequent basis. Ask them, "Am I getting it right?"

□ **Own it.** If you're not getting something right, if you're not performing to standard, what is your plan? Don't blame somebody or something else for your shortcomings. You need to own your own performance and your plan to address it.

□ **Do it.** Do what you need to do to meet a standard of high performance in your job. It's the only way to really earn the right to contribute. There's no easy way. You can't talk or bluff your way through.

□ **Report back.** Communicate your progress to your line manager. Don't wait for him or her to come to you—it may never happen! Take charge and make sure you know how you are doing in the eyes of the organization.

8

Conclusion: Make It a Way of Life!

"Of course our genes, circumstances, and environments matter very much, and they shape us significantly. Yet there remains an inner zone in which we are sovereign, unless we abdicate. In this zone lives the essence of our individuality and our personal accountability."

Neal A. Maxwell, educator, theologian

To rely on the organization to engage you is like keeping all your money in cash when you're surrounded by high inflation. After a while, you don't have much left. Like it or not, you live in a turbulent world. Just take a minute to inhale your surroundings. Things are very different in the twenty-first century. The U.S. military, for example, came up with the concept of VUCA to characterize the current environment:

V = Volatility. The nature, depth, breadth, patterns, and speed of change.

U = Uncertainty. The lack of clarity, predictability, and probability of events and outcomes.

C = Complexity. The multiplex of variables, relationships, and timing.

A = Ambiguity. The deception and confusion of cause and effect that overwhelm our ability to interpret and respond.

The impact of VUCA cuts both ways: it offers greater opportunity for those who take the initiative, and less opportunity for those who curl up and wait for things to happen. If VUCA sends one clear message, it admonishes us to take charge of our professional lives if we want to have any hope of directing the outcome. That's really the message of this book. But it's an uphill battle. As a culture, we're still fighting the impoverished idea that the organization is primarily responsible for engaging the employee. And yet this idea has been upended by reality. It still needs to be upended in the hearts and minds of millions of people. That's a hard thing to do. The most difficult prison to escape has no cement walls or iron bars. It's simply the self-imposed incarceration of the human will. The galvanic power to become highly engaged lies within the individual.

How do you fight against the uncertainty and the demoralizing forces of the economy? There's only one thing you can do: make empowering choices and take personal accountability for those choices. Become a self-determining individual. Move from a state of dependency to independence. Deterministic and paternalistic ideas about engagement are simply wrong. Sometimes organizations limit our progress. But more often we limit our own progress by putting a personal firewall around us. We stymie our own aspirations by the choices we make.

In *The Devil's Dictionary*, Ambrose Bierce defines the term responsibility this way: "RESPONSIBILITY, n. A detachable burden easily shifted to the shoulders of God, Fate, Fortune, Luck or one's neighbor. In the days of astrology it was customary to unload it upon a star."[1] Disengaged people often shift responsibility this way. They expect and wait, and they wait and expect. It's easier to change yourself than an entire organization. The option always remains, however, as Samuel Johnson said, "To do nothing is in every man's power."

Many people simply exist in organizations. They're not excited about life. They're not doing all they could do. They're shipwrecked on the reefs of dependency, waiting for the organization to rescue them. We have no evidence that this strategy works. We do have evidence that such an approach can become a narcotic welfare system to the individual. It has been said that the unexamined life is not worth living. Neither is the disengaged life.

The late track star Steve Prefontaine once said, "To give less than your best is to sacrifice the gift." What gift? The gift of who and what you are, the gift of your life and contribution.

You are caught in the middle of a transformation—a transformation about what it means to be an employee, to have a job, and to add value to an organization. We have put forward the case that employee engagement is now and forever your primary responsibility. You will have to come to your own conclusion on that point.

The reality is that fewer than one in four employees are buoyant and afloat with a high level of engagement. The rest are doing other things—waiting, grousing, looking for the next shiny fad, or whatever. It doesn't really matter what they're doing if they're not exercising their prerogative to be highly engaged. And it's not just the individual employee who is misguided. Organizations are too. We still observe many organizations resorting to money and gimmicks as their primary engagement strategy. Does splashing the cash really engage employees for the long term? Does it really draw out passion and discretionary effort?

> *"Those who say 'yes' are rewarded by the adventures they have. Those who say 'no' are rewarded by the safety they attain."*
>
> Keith Johnstone, improv theater expert

Get Out of Your Own Way

We need a shift in mindset. Engagement, like self-esteem, is impossible without the responsibility of significant personal effort and earned achievement. Consequently, the six drivers of high engagement are not easy to apply. In our study of highly engaged individuals, we have yet to identify a single shortcut. And yet we do witness individuals who sustain high engagement throughout their entire professional lives. We see individuals applying the six drivers and delivering astounding results for themselves and the organizations they work for.

> *"There is a time in every man's education when he arrives at the conviction that envy is ignorance; that imitation is suicide; that he must take himself for better or worse as his portion; that though the wide universe is full of good, no kernel of nourishing corn can come to him but through his toil bestowed on that plot of ground which is given to him to till."*
>
> Ralph Waldo Emerson

What Is Your Responsibility?

Can we assume that your employer will do all it can to support your success? Should we say that you have an important reciprocal obligation to be highly engaged, and you should do it when the organization does its part? The answer is a resounding no. Don't assume your employer will do anything. That kind of assumption is the very thing we're talking about. That assumption kills engagement and puts you on the path of entitlement and professional welfare. For your own sake and for the sake of others, here's what you can do:

- **Release your discretionary effort now.** Don't turn professional life into a miserly exchange in which there's a quid pro quo for everything you do. Invest ahead of the organization. The organization may reward you tenfold. It may not. Even if the organization does not fully appreciate your contribution, do your best. You will take your experience with you. No one can strip you of the hard-won lessons you learn and the experience you gain. They are yours forever.

- **Eat change for breakfast.** Change will choose you even if you don't choose it. And it always requires two things: the performance of work and the absorption of stress. There are no stormproof companies, and there are no sources of competitive advantage that last forever. It's all ice. The only question is the rate of the melt. The forces of change will come from inside and outside the organization. It's all VUCA as far as the eye can see. Compression and acceleration will be the dominant themes of market behavior. But none of that should surprise you. "Change is to be expected and that support for change is a condition of long-term employment."[2]

- **Be grateful and happy.** You are not entitled to a crabby, peevish attitude. You have an obligation to be positive, encouraging, and helpful. Even if you have a poor leader as a boss, you're still better off making the biggest contribution you can. Keep in mind that you're developing a rhythm and cadence to your professional life. Don't let the weaknesses and dysfunctions of the organization set the tone for you. Aristotle said, "We are what we repeatedly do." Bring some enthusiasm and see what damage you can do.

- **Make things better.** Once you have built a personal platform of credibility, you have the right to put something on the table. Challenge the status quo where it makes sense. Manage risk and don't be careless, but try to make things better. A little swashbuckling can be a good thing. You may not be the most creative and innovative person, but if you simply want to improve things and are looking for an opportunity, those opportunities are more likely to appear. If we take you to a street corner, for instance, you will look at the passing traffic and not think much of it. But if we ask you to find the green cars, you will immediately begin to see them.

- **Be accountable.** It's amazing how long it takes people to stop making excuses. Isn't it interesting that the human mind has an infinite capacity to rationalize? When reality doesn't meet our expectations, we can escape to never-never land. We can accept or deny. We can embrace reality or fashion a new version. Because humans hate discord between themselves and reality, they tend to change themselves or pretend to change reality. We can tell ourselves a soothing story. We have become very good at telling ourselves soothing stories, and we tend to spend an enormously long time doing it. In fact, we often wait for the impending crisis to hit before we are ready to throw away our soothing story. It's a blessed day when we choose to be fully accountable for our own performance.

- **Use the delete key.** Push it not only for negative feedback that would discourage you, but also for gratuitous praise that would lead you to falsely believe in your own superiority. Both strains of input are dangerous. If you want to develop the courage to be wrong, throw out the sentimental slush as well as the harmful criticism.

What's the Organization's Responsibility?

Engaging employees has become a more difficult challenge. Some experts forecast a tsunami of employee defection in the future. That's an exaggeration, but the problem is real. Fortunately, some organizations are entering a new era of enlightenment. In greater numbers, leaders are beginning to shed the mindset, values, and beliefs of an industrial age that have outlived their usefulness. At the same time, we have also entered a new era of entitlement on the part of some employees. It's not necessarily that they expect a BMW 3 Series and a condo on their first day of work, but many want to be catered to. That doesn't work. Here are a few suggestions for leaders and organizations:

☐ **Promise and deliver effort.** Many organizations would love to offer loyalty and job security, but that's not possible. VUCA simply won't allow it. As Jeff Jarvis said, "Loyalty from employer to employee died in my lifetime."[3] So what do you do? Promise effort. Make an honest declaration to your employees that you're going to do all you can, and you're going to ask for their help. Organizations can't find their employees' motivation. No one can do that. Engagement is inexorably connected to self-esteem, and self-esteem is connected to esteemable acts. Engagement isn't free. It carries with it the responsibility of personal effort, of work, of exertion sustained over time. It has its price. But if the employees believe the organization will make a good faith effort on their behalf, that goes an awful long way.

☐ **Be a leader of conscience.** Don't try to hide behind title, position, and authority. That's a cop-out, and it's not lost on anyone paying attention. Either lead with genuine concern for the growth and development of your people or let someone else take the helm. In the global age, we are fast reaching the point of diminishing returns with command and control management. Knowledge workers in particular ignore it, disengage, or opt out.

☐ **Give permission to challenge.** The predominant vibe in many organizations is compliance. Get rid of needless rigidity and stupid rules. In fact, let your highly engaged employees hack through the bureaucracy. Let them challenge the status quo. Let them challenge you. Recognize them when they do.

☐ **Coach the individual.** If you can't offer job security, what specifically can you do to help your people professionally? First, give them more flexibility. If you can find a way to flex, do it. Second, give them more emotional support. It costs nothing but a little time and energy. Sadly, many employees expect less real career support. See if you can exceed their expectations—

not necessarily with more resources, but with personal coaching time. Increase your face time. Get out of the office, off the phone, and out from behind the computer monitor. Give your attention freely and abundantly to the individual.

☐ **Win on imagination.** David MacLeod and Nita Clarke put it this way: "In a world where most factors of production are increasingly standardized, where a production line or the goods on a supermarket shelf are much the same the world over, employee engagement *is* the difference that *makes* the difference—and could make all the difference as we face the realities of globalised competition."[4] In a globalizing world, where time frames are compressed, where business models are quickly overtaken, where competitive advantage is elusive and fleeting, and where disruptive forces may exert themselves at any time, organizational failure will increasingly become a failure of imagination. The companies most at risk are the ones with unengaged people—unmotivated, uninspired, and uncommitted, and therefore unimaginative. They will fail on imagination—not because they don't have any, but because leaders are unable to draw it out. The conclusion that we unavoidably come to is that strategy matters less than it did, at least in the sense that an organization can ride a long-term business model for long-term growth and profitability. Fewer markets allow that anymore. Further, we have only limited visibility into the future. We have to look into the fog and do the best that we can now, embracing the uncertainty that we may need to adjust and adapt at any time. This is a different way of leading an organization. It requires dynamic learning, dynamic planning, and dynamic execution. Think about how unfit and unmatched the old industrial model is to this requirement. If you can help your employees become more engaged, you can win on imagination.

Notes

Chapter 1

1. Shirley S. Wang, "Is Happiness Overrated?," *Wall Street Journal*, March 15, 2011, D6.

2. Elton Mayo, *Hawthorne and the Western Electric Company: The Social Problems of an Industrial Civilization* (New York: Routledge, 1949).

3. As it turns out, employees were responding more to the fact that they knew they were being studied.

4. Thomas H. Davenport, Jeanne Harris, and Jeremy Shapiro, "Competing on Talent Analytics," *Harvard Business Review*, October 2010, 1.

5. See, for instance, William H. Macey and Benjamin Schneider, "The Meaning of Employee Engagement," *Industrial and Organizational Psychology* 1 (2008); and Paul M. Mastrangelo, "Will Employee Engagement Be Hijacked or Reengineered?," *Genesee Survey Services*, 2008.

6. The major engagement studies include those conducted by the Gallup Organization, Towers-Watson, Hewitt Associates, BlessingWhite, and Mercer. Some studies put the percentage of highly engaged at much lower levels. For example, the Corporate Leadership Council's major study in 2004 pegged the percentage of highly engaged at just 11 percent. See Corporate Leadership Council 2004 Employee Engagement Survey.

7. Tory Johnson, "Be Your Own Boss! Tips for Starting a Small Business in 2011," January 3, 2011, accessed January 4, 2011, http://abcnews.go.com/Business/JobClub/boss-tips-starting -small-business–2011/story?id=12525165.

8. Richard M. Ryan and Edward L. Deci, "Self-Determination Theory and the Facilitation of Intrinsic Motivation, Social Development, and Well Being," *American Psychologist*, January 2000, 69.

9. See Julie Gebauer and Don Lowman, *Closing the Engagement Gap: How Great Companies Unlock Employee Potential for Superior Results* (New York: Portfolio, 2008).

10. Jack and Suzy Welch, "A Healthy Company?," *Bloomberg Businessweek*, May 3, 2006, http://www.businessweek.com /mediacenter/podcasts/welchway/welchway_05_03_06.htm.

11. Employee engagement based on intrinsic motivation can trace its roots to classic motivation theorists and their seminal works, including Abraham Maslow, "A Theory of Human Motivation" (1943); Robert W. White, *Ego and Reality in Psychoanalytic Theory* (1963); Douglas McGregor, *The Human Side of Enterprise* (1960); Frederick Hertzberg, *Work and the Nature of Man* (Cleveland: World Publishing, 1966); C. Alderfer, "An Empirical Test of a New Theory of Human Needs," *Organizational Behavior and Human Performance* 4 (1969): 143–175; and W. Edwards Deming, *The New Economics for Industry, Government and Education* (Cambridge, MA: Institute of Technology Center for Advanced Engineering Study, 1993).

Chapter 2

1. "U.S. Teen Mobile Report: Calling Yesterday, Texting Today, Using Apps Tomorrow," *NielsenWire*, http://blog.nielsen.com /nielsenwire/online_mobile/u-s-teen-mobile-report-calling -yesterday-texting-today-using-apps-tomorrow/.

2. Ben Parr, "Average Teenager Sends 3,339 Texts per Month," Mashable.com, http:// www.cnn.com/2010/TECH/mobile/10/15 /teen.texting.mashable/index.html.

3. Jamie Cooper-Hohn, "Organization: The Next Big Innovation," *McKinsey Quarterly*, November 2011, http://whatmatters .mckinseydigital.com/social_innovation/organization-the-next -big-innovation.

4. Roman Friedrich, Michael Peterson, and Alex Koster, "The Rise of Generation C: How to Prepare for the Connected Generation's Transformation of the Consumer and Business Landscape," *Strategy+Business*, Booz & Company, February 23, 2011, http://www.strategy-business.com/article/11110?gko =64e54.

5. Intel Fact Sheet, "2011 State of Mobile Etiquette: Parents, Children and Their Relationship with Mobile Technology," http://newsroom.intel.com/docs/DOC–1883.

6. Karim R. Lakhani and Robert G. Wolf, "Why Hackers Do What They Do: Understanding Motivation and Effort in Free/ Open Source Software Projects," in *Perspectives on Free and Open Software*, ed. J. Feller, B. Fitzgerald, S. Hissam, and K. Lakhani (Cambridge, MA: MIT Press, 2005), 3, 12.

7. Personal interviews with Phillip Meade conducted by Shane Cragun, September 2011.

Chapter 3

1. Mike Swift, "YouTube Shifts from Google Offshoot to Strategic Model," *Deseret News*, March 3, 2011, A11.

2. "The Multigenerational Workforce: Opportunity for Competitive Success," *Society for Human Resource Management*, January–March 2009, 4–5.

3. See, for example, IMB Global Business Services, "Unlocking the DNA of the Adaptable Workforce: The Global Human Capital Study 2008."

4. Michelle Conlin, "Smashing the Clock," *Bloomberg Businessweek*, December 11, 2006, http://www.businessweek.com /magazine/content/06_50/b4013001.htm; Tony Schwartz, Jean

Gomes, and Catherine McCarthy, *The Way We're Working Isn't Working* (New York: Free Press, 2010), 231–232; Cali Ressler and Jody Thompson, *Why Work Sucks and How to Fix It* (New York: Penguin Group, 2008), 3–8.

5. Douglas T. Hall coined the concept of a "protean career" in his book *Careers in Organizations* (Pacific Palisades, CA: Goodyear Publishing, 1976).

6. Anya Kamenetz, "The Four-Year Career," *Fast Company.* February 2012, 74.

7. Derby Cox, "How Long Is the Future?," interview of Eric Schmidt, November 15, 2011, http://smartblogs.com/leadership /2011/11/15/vip-corner-eric-schmidt-asks-how-long-is-the -future/.

8. Nadira A. Hira, "You Raised Them, Now Manage Them," *Fortune,* May 28, 2007, 38–46.

9. Sue Shellenbarger, "Can't Pick a College Major? Create One," *Wall Street Journal,* November 17, 2010.

10. Ibid.

11. Anya Kamenetz, *DIY U: Edupunks, Edupreneurs and the Coming Transformation of Higher Education* (White River Junction, VT: Chelsea Green Publishing, 2010).

12. BlessingWhite, *The State of Employee Engagement,* 2008, 1.

13. Ed Frauenheim, "On the Clock but Off on Their Own: Pet-Project Programs Set to Gain Wider Acceptance," April 1, 2010, www.singlearticles.com, http://www.singlearticles.com /on-the-clock-but-a1551.html,

14. Jena McGregor, "How to Make a Smart Lateral Career Move," *Fortune,* October 13, 2011, http://management.fortune.cnn .com/2011/10/13/career-lateral-move/.

15. Daniel H. Pink, *Drive: The Surprising Truth About What Motivates Us* (New York: Riverhead Books, 2009), 92–98.

16. Manoj Jasra, "50% of Google's Products Came from 20% Time (and Other Facts and Figures)," Web Analytics Blog, www.webanalyticsworld.net.

17. Pink, *Drive*, 115.

18. Ann March, "The Art of Work," *Fast Company*, August 2005, http://www.fastcompany.com/magazine/97/art-of-work.html.

19. Karim R. Lakhani and Robert G. Wolf, "Why Hackers Do What They Do: Understanding Motivation and Effort in Free/Open Source Software Projects," in *Perspectives on Free and Open Software*, ed. J. Feller, B. Fitzgerald, S. Hissam, and K. Lakhani (Cambridge, MA: MIT Press, 2005), 3, 12.

20. Alan M. Webber, "Danger: Toxic Company," *Fast Company*, October 31, 1998, http://www.fastcompany.com/magazine/19/toxic.html.

21. Pink, *Drive*, 31.

22. Tim Sanders, *The Likeablity Factor* (New York: Three Rivers Press, 2005), 47.

23. Frederick Herzberg, "One More Time: How Do You Motivate Employees," *Harvard Business Review*, September-October 1987, p. 6.

24. Sanders, *Likeability Factor.*

25. Telework Trendlines 2009, data collected by the Dieringer Research Group, published by World at Work, February 2009.

26. Quoted in *Harvard Business Essentials: Managing Creativity and Innovation* (Boston: Harvard Business School Press, 2003), 109.

27. Tony Schwarz, Jean Gomes, Catherine McCarthy, *The Way We're Working Isn't Working* (New York: Free Press, 2010), 230.

28. Ibid., 231.

29. Beverly L. Kaye, *Love It, Don't Leave It: 26 Ways to Get What You Want at Work* (San Francisco: Berrett-Koehler Publishers, 2003), 12.

30. Dana E. Friedman, "Supervisors Guide to Flexibility," Families and Work Institute, 3.

31. Ibid., 4.

Chapter 4

1. Henry Sauerman and Wesley Cohen, "What Makes Them Tick? Employee Motives and Firm Innovation," NBER Working Paper no. 14443, October 2008.

2. John Tagg, *The Learning Paradigm* (San Francisco: Jossey-Bass, 2003), 54.

3. Timothy R. Clark, "Are You an Aggressive, Self-Directed Learner," *Deseret News*, January 24, 2011, B2.

4. Tracey J. Shors, "Saving New Brain Cells," *Scientific American*, March 2009, 47.

5. Isaac Disraeli, *Curiosities of Literature* (New York: William Pearson & Company, 1835), 28.

6. Scott C. Beardsley, Bradford C. Johnson, and James M. Manyika, "Competitive Advantage from Better Interactions," *McKinsey Quarterly*, no. 2 (2006): 53–63; Michael A. Lapré and Luk N. Van Wassenhove, "Learning Across Lines: The Secret to More Efficient Factories," *Harvard Business Review*, October 2002, 107–111.

7. The section draws heavily from Timothy R. Clark and Conrad A. Gottfredson, *Special Research Report: In Search of Learning Agility: Assessing Progress from 1957 to 2008*, TRClark and ASTD Research, September 2008.

8. Mark Blazey, *Insights to Performance Excellence 2009–2010: An Inside Look at the 2009–2010 Baldridge Award Criteria*, 17.

9. See www.emc.com/collateral/analyst-reports/expanding-digital-idc-white-paper.pdf. See also Kathleen Parker, "Turn Off,

Tune Out, Drop In," *Washington Post*, December 2008, www
.washingtonpost.com/wp-dyn/content/article/2009/03/31
/AR2009033103318.html.

10. Michael S. Malone, "The Next American Frontier," *Wall Street Journal*, May 19, 2008, A15.

11. Please note the importance and need for spaced or distributed learning. See Lila Davachi, Tobias Kiefer, David Rock and Lisa Rock, "Learning That Lasts Through the Ages," *Neuro-Leadership Journal* 3 (2010).

12. Adam Bryant, "A Near-Death Event, a Corporate Rite of Passage," *New York Times*, August 1, 2009, http://www .nytimes.com/2009/08/02/business/02corner.html.

13. Interview with Cael Sanderson conducted on April 13, 2011, by Timothy R. Clark.

14. Alan Fine, *You Already Know How to Be Great* (New York: Portfolio, 2010), 6.

15. "Blueprint for Jobs in the 21st Century," HR Policy Association, April 2011, 36, http://www.hrpolicy.org/downloads/2011/11–30 _Blueprint_for_Jobs.pdf.

Chapter 5

1. "Tour de France a Spectacle of Extreme Human Performance, Says Physiologist," June 20, 2011, http://www.news .ku.edu/2011/june/30/tourdefrance.shtml.

2. Sam Marye Lewis, "Cycling in the Zone," Athletic Insight, 2011.

3. Susan Jackson and Mihaly Csikszentmihalyi, *Flow in Sports: The Keys to Optimal Experiences and Performances* (Champaign, IL: Human Kinetics, 1999).

4. Gary Hopkins, "How Can Teachers Develop Students' Motivation and Success?," interview with Carol Dweck for *Education World*, 2005, http://www.educationworld.com/a_issues/chat /chat010.shtml.

5. Edmund S. Phelps, "Dynamic Capitalism," *Wall Street Journal*, October 10, 2006, http://economistsview.typepad.com/economistsview/2006/10/phelps_dynamic_.html.

6. *Effective effort* is a concept used interchangeably with the term *deliberate practice*, which is also quite similar to the concepts of metacognition and executive function. It is defined as "considerable, specific, and sustained efforts to do something you can't do well." See K. A. Ericsson, M. J. Pritula, and E. T. Cokely, "The Making of an Expert," *Harvard Business Review*, July 2007.

Chapter 6

1. Peter F. Drucker, "My Life as a Knowledge Worker," February 1, 1997, accessed December 15, 2011, http://www.inc.com/magazine/19970201/1169.html.

2. Frederick Herzberg, "One More Time: How Do You Motivate Employees?," *Harvard Business Review*, September–October 1987, reprint, 9.

3. Edward L. Deci, Richard M. Ryan, and Richard Koestner, "A Meta-Analytic Review of Experiments Examining the Effects of Extrinsic Rewards on Intrinsic Motivation," *Psychological Bulletin* 125, no. 6 (1999): 659.

4. Daniel H. Pink, *Drive: The Surprising Truth About What Motivates Us* (New York: Riverhead Books, 2009), 8.

5. Kim Girard, "Recovering from the Need to Achieve," Harvard Business School, Working Knowledge, June 27, 2011, 1.

6. Anthony Daniels, "The Barbarians Inside Britain's Gates," *Wall Street Journal*, August 15, 2011, A13.

7. Jeffrey M. Schwartz, *The Mind and the Brain: Neuroplasticity and the Power of Mental Force* (New York: Harper Perennial, 2002). See also www.welcome.ac.uk/News/2004/Features/WTX032958.htm.

8. Arthur C. Clark, "Superiority," in *Expedition to Earth* (London: Orbit, 1981).

9. Rob Norton, "The Thought Leader Interview: Sylvia Nasar," *Strategy+Business* 64. August 23, 2011, http://m.strategy -business.com/article/11311?gko=72d26.

10. Bill Walton, *Bill Walton on BYU vs. San Diego State*, February 28, 2011, XX 1099 AM Sports Radio, San Diego.

11. Teresa M. Amabile and Steven J. Kramer, "Inner Work Life: Understanding the Subtext of Business Performance," *Harvard Business Review*, May 2007, 12.

Chapter 7

1. Clayton M. Christensen, "How Will You Measure Your Life?," *Harvard Business Review*, July 2010, http://hbr.org/2010/07 /how-will-you-measure-your-life/ar/1.

2. Walter Isaacson, *Steve Jobs* (New York: Simon & Schuster, 2011), chapter 42, "Legacy: The Brightest Heaven of Invention."

3. Douglas C. Heiner, "The Korean War as Seen Through the Eyes of First Lieutenant Douglas C. Heiner, M.D.: Military Service July 1, 1951 to June 30, 1953," shared with Conrad Gottfredson on June 6, 2011.

4. See Leigh Branham, *The 7 Hidden Reasons Employees Leave* (New York: AMACOM, 2005).

5. Ibid.

Chapter 8

1. Ambrose Bierce and Chas Bufe, *The Devil's Dictionaries* (Tucson, AZ: Sharp Press, 1995).

2. Christopher G. Worley and Edward E. Lawler III, "Designing Organizations That Are Built to Change," *MIT Sloan Management Review* 48, no. 1 (fall 2008), 19.

3. Jeff Jarvis, *What Would Google Do?* (New York: Collins Business, 2009), 57.

4. David MacLeod and Nita Clarke, *Engaging for Success: Enhancing Performance Through Employee Engagement* (London: Crown, 2009), 4.

Index

About the Authors

Timothy R. Clark is founder and CEO of TRClark LLC, a consultancy that provides advisory services in strategy, large-scale change and transformation, executive development, and employee engagement. He also writes the syndicated column "On Leadership" for the *Deseret News* and is a powerful and highly acclaimed keynote speaker. He is a global authority in the field of change leadership and organizational transformation.

Clark is the author of the critically acclaimed book *Epic Change: How to Lead Change in the Global Age* (John Wiley/Jossey-Bass), which CEO Refresher named the top management book on the subject of change of 2008. Stephen R. Covey calls *Epic Change* "absolutely brilliant material," and Dave Ulrich of the University of Michigan calls it a "neo-classic." He is also the author of *The Leadership Test: Will You Pass?* (2009), which Christopher Germann at Gartner Research calls "simple, elegant, and profound." Some of his clients include Accenture, Accor, American Express, AmerisourceBergen, Boston Scientific, Chevron, CIGNA, Disney, Dow Chemical, Eli Lilly, Environmental Protection Agency, Freedom Communications, HCA, Honeywell, Idaho National Laboratory, Intel, Internal Revenue Service, John Hopkins University, Ketchum, Lake Forest Hospital, Medical City Dallas Hospital, Microsoft, NASA, Northwestern Memorial Hospital, Sprint, Stanford University, U.S. Department of Treasury, Vancouver Island Health Authority, and Wells Fargo Bank.

Clark earned a doctor's degree in international politics from Oxford University and was both a Fulbright and a British Research Scholar. He also earned a master's degree in government and economics from the University of Utah. As an undergraduate at

Brigham Young University, he was named a first-team Academic All-American football player and completed a triple degree.

Conrad Gottfredson has 30 years of experience helping organizations develop effective leaders, learn at the speed of change, optimize their learning and performance systems, and manage their knowledge/content capital. He holds a PhD in Instructional Psychology and Technology from Brigham Young University and is considered a global authority on organizational learning and performance support. His consulting work has helped governments, nonprofits, and multinational organizations employ emerging technologies and methodologies wisely to help people achieve personal and organizational goals. He has pioneered methodologies for developing and delivering learning at the moment of need to those who need it, when they need it, in the language and form they require, from a single source of content. His unique collaborative consulting style has helped him develop simple, practical solutions to the common challenges facing organizations at all levels. He is the author with Bob Mosher of *Innovative Performance Support* (McGraw-Hill, 2011).

Kendall Lyman is a founding principal of The Cornerstone Group, a consulting firm known for leading-edge approaches to business strategy, process design, leadership development, and large-scale cultural change that produce sustainable and tangible results. He is a member of the Duke Corporate Education Global Learning Resource Network. Kendall has worked across diverse industries, such as oil and gas, financial services, pharmaceutical, lodging, government, and manufacturing. He has consulted internationally on projects in Europe, Asia, and Africa, and he speaks fluent Spanish. Kendall's work with clients has been recognized nationally. The Navy Postal Group in Washington, D.C., won the Federal Mail Center Excellence Award; the Norfolk Naval Shipyard won the Virginia State Quality Award; and Kendall's participation in the work to split InterContinental Hotels Group from its parent received the ASTD Excellence in Practice Award. Other clients include Kellogg's, Suncor, Eli Lilly, Sun Life, Auto-Trader, Medtronic, Graymont, National MS Society, Shea Homes, NASA Kennedy Space Center, Merck, Nationwide, the Atlanta Journal Constitution, and Carlson Companies. Kendall is coauthor of *The Business Strategy Audit: A Company Self-Assessment* and a white paper series entitled *A Case for Change Management*.

Shane Cragun is a founding principal of The Cornerstone Group. Shane has consulted across the globe in diverse industries such as financial services, technology, manufacturing, professional services, oil and gas, government, hotel and lodging, and home building. His projects have received several awards, the most recent of which is the J. D. Power Award for Best Customer Service. Selected clients include Citigroup, Yale University, Motel 6, Wells Fargo, EDS, Lucent, NASA, Shea Homes, KPMG, Yokosuka Japan U.S. Naval Shipyard Repair Facility, Merck, Mobil Oil Chalmette Refinery, Abu Dhabi Investment Authority, and Air National Guard. Earlier in his career, he served as the VP and GM over Franklin Covey's consulting and training division where he oversaw all external training and consulting personnel nationally. Shane is a faculty member of the Duke University Corporate Education Resource Network.

Scott Savage is a senior consultant at FranklinCovey, an international sales and consulting organization. For the past 31 years, Scott has consulted tens of thousands of business leaders at many of the world's largest professional service, high-tech, and manufacturing concerns and many federal agencies. His client list includes AkzoNobel, Accenture, Arthur D. Little, Booz Allen Hamilton, Booz & Co., CIA, Computer Associates, Crowe Horworth, Deloitte, Department of Defense, Hewlett-Packard, Hitachi Consulting, KPMG, Microsoft, Motorola, Nike, Oracle, Panduit, Quest Diagnostics, Siemens, Symantec, Texaco, Underwriters Laboratories, Verizon, Visa, and Whirlpool. In addition to bringing thought leadership, consulting, and training to the world of leadership, change management, and sales leadership, he is also a widely sought after keynote speaker.

Mike Baer is a senior consultant with FranklinCovey. He also coauthors a national business development e-newsletter that is delivered to organizations, sales leaders, and business development consultants each week. Mike has also taught and consulted hundreds of business development leaders in several large professional services firms across North America.

Tobias Kiefer is director of global learning and development, Booz & Co., Munich, Germany. He is a leader, speaker, trainer, and coach working at the intersection of talent management, consulting, and neuroscience. His passion is to guide individuals and teams to be more effective in order to focus on the essentials and make better decisions and in order to achieve better results—both professionally and personally. As former athlete and talent scout for young biathletes, he set the tone for constantly aspiring for new goals instead of accepting the status quo. He has led multiple large-scale strategic projects in the financial services industry, transportation, and real estate across different cultures.

Alistair Aitchison is managing director and a senior partner with Emenex, a consulting and training organization in Oxfordshire in the United Kingdom. Alistair was previously vice president of marketing and sales development across EMEA for Novell. Prior to that, Alistair had five years within the management development program of Air Products and Chemicals in the UK, Germany, and Netherlands and two years with ICI in the UK. At Emenex Alistair delivers solutions in the areas of employee engagement, talent and change management, and sales management, coaching, and measurement. Some of his clients include Intel, Molson Coors, Acronis, GMAC RFC, DC Thomson, BP, Dubai Properties, ADCO, Extreme Networks, KCI, and Ciena. Alistair received his bachelor's degree from Edinburgh University and completed his MBA at the Marriott School of Management at Brigham Young University.

The Engagement Mindset Support Center

We hope you've enjoyed reading *The Employee Engagement Mindset*. What's the next step? Whether you're a member of a Fortune 500 corporation or a garage-based entrepreneur, the next step is to turn an event into a process. That means applying the six drivers to increase and sustain your own engagement.

To help you in that process, we've created "The Engagement Mindset Support Center." The support center is a virtual center that helps you transfer and apply what you've learned. We want to help you close the "knowing vs. doing" gap. You know a lot about the six drivers of engagement. Now it's time to put the drivers into action.

The Support Center provides the following kinds of help for each of the six drivers of engagement:

- online tools
- video illustrations and explanations
- assessments
- discussion boards
- podcasts
- success stories
- live web training with authors
- e-Learning course offerings
- public training course offerings
- special events calendar
- in-house training and certification information
- retreats and keynotes calendar

Come visit the center any time at
www.engagementmindset.com.

CPSIA information can be obtained at www.ICGtesting.com
Printed in the USA
LVOW10*0504241114

415276LV00009B/136/P